# Spiritual Family Trees

## Finding Your Faith Community's Roots

## Barbara Wendland and Larry W. Easterling

AN ALBAN INSTITUTE PUBLICATION

Copyright © 2001 by the Alban Institute. All rights reserved.

This material may not be photocopied or reproduced in any way without written permission.

Library of Congress Catalog Card Number 2001094863

ISBN 1-56699-249-4

# CONTENTS

# PREFACE

After unsuccessfully trying to find a book about spiritual family trees, to mention in her monthly newsletter, Barbara woke in the middle of the night, thinking, "Maybe Larry and I should collaborate on a book about it." The next day, without having heard about her middle-of-the-night thoughts, Larry sent her an e-mail, saying: "Since there evidently aren't any such books, maybe we should write one." *Spiritual Family Trees* is the result.

We are immensely grateful to Alban Institute managing editor David Lott for his continual active involvement in the writing process. He made innumerable helpful observations and suggestions and always surrounded them with encourage-ment. We're also grateful to Barbara's daughter, Carol Wendland, for her perceptive analysis and helpful suggestions.

Our thanks go, too, to our spouses, Julia Rogers and Erroll Wendland, for their support while we wrote and rewrote. And to the members of the Sunday School class in which we shared spiritual family trees together, the Searchers Class of First United Methodist Church in Temple, Texas, we send our heartfelt "Thank you!" for encouraging us and letting us include bits of your spiritual histories in our book. We also thank the other lay people and pastors whose tree-sharing experiences we describe here.

Finally, Larry sends his thanks to all the Clinical Pastoral Education students

v

with whom he has been privileged to journey during the past 20 years. He feels that whatever he may have taught them has been returned tenfold in rich learning and relationships. And to Anna, his daughter, Larry would like to acknowledge her challenge of integrating her minister father, for better or worse, into her spiritual family tree. May God be kind to her in her journey.

BARBARA WENDLAND
Temple, Texas

LARRY W. EASTERLING
Oak Lawn, Illinois

# CHAPTER 1

# Finding a New Family

I t's one of the best things we've ever done," says a Sunday School class member.

"I understand a lot more now, about who I'm with and why we each have the ideas we have," another adds.

"There was a sacredness about it, a sanctity that was very clear," says a pastor.

"After this experience," says the president of a group whose members had previously been at each other's throats, "you feel like they are all your family. It was so exciting to see them bond together."

These enthusiastic reactions came from sharing what we call "spiritual family trees." Sharing these trees is a way of sharing spiritual histories in a religious group in order to build community. In other settings the diagrams central to this process are called "genograms." They are similar to the family tree diagrams that genealogists use to show how family members through several generations are related.

If you've developed that kind of family tree to show your family's genealogy, you've probably had to search for information about earlier generations. You may have had to ask older family members about some of their experiences. You probably had to get information about family members who are no longer living, including some who died before you were born. In this search you're likely to have discovered experiences and

1

feelings that strongly influenced family members' choices about who to marry, where to live, or what occupation to follow. You may have found the origin of longstanding family conflicts. You may have turned up all sorts of interesting stories you'd never heard before. You may have even become aware of physical characteristics and occupational choices that have reappeared generation after generation within your family.

If you have a genetic disease or deformity in your family history, you may have consulted a genetic counselor to learn how to prevent that ailment in your children. Or if a harmful pattern of behavior appears in successive generations of your family, you may have consulted a therapist for help in identifying that pattern and stopping it.

The kinds of information that genealogists, genetic counselors, and therapists record in genograms, however, tell only part of your story. What would you do if you wanted to trace your spiritual history?

## Sharing Our Spiritual Histories

In our Sunday School class we used genograms in tracing and sharing our spiritual histories. We looked at how religious practices, attitudes, and beliefs had been passed down through our families, often without members' being aware of what was happening. We looked at how family members and other people close to us had influenced our spiritual growth and church involvement, for good or for ill.

We'd previously shared personal feelings and experiences often in class, especially when a member was facing a crisis or a happy new experience. Some of us see each other regularly outside of class sessions—at work, in social activities, or in other church groups. A few class members are close personal friends. So even before we shared spiritual family trees, most of us thought we knew each other reasonably well.

As it turns out, we didn't. Sharing

spiritual family trees gave us surprising new insight into the feelings and beliefs of class members, even those we thought we knew best.

We heard about church experiences that had strongly influenced class members' feelings about the church. Members who had found worship services boring in childhood, but had been required to attend them, saw the need to make worship interesting for children and teenagers. Members who had known sexually promiscuous or financially irresponsible pastors had come to distrust all pastors. Class members who had seen church leadership positions given only to the wealthiest church members, or had seen the top positions given to blatant adulterers or corrupt businesspeople or politicians, had come to believe that many church members were hypocrites. Sharing our stories also made us aware of class members' tender spots, those personal topics that we needed to treat gently. When we heard about members' divorces, those of us with good marriages

realized that we should avoid glib claims that everyone should marry and stay married. We realized that careless mention of miscarriage, suicide, or tragic death could needlessly revive painful memories.

We saw, too, why some class members preferred certain kinds of study materials and methods. At one time, these materials and methods had led to rewarding—even life-changing—religious experiences for those members.

Gaining such insight about personal and church-related experience knit us together as a group, to an extent we hadn't imagined before. Seeing the similarities and differences in family background and religious experience brought us closer. It also made us care more about what was happening in each other's lives. After hearing a class member's spiritual family tree, when that member reported the death of a relative who had played a crucial role in his or her religious upbringing, we knew why that death was of special concern. We knew what to ask and

3

what kind of support to offer. Conversation with that class member could now be more than the superficialities that would otherwise have been all we knew to say. We had become a real group instead of separate individuals who happened to show up at the same place on Sunday mornings.

We're a small group: 12 to 15 most Sundays. Most of us have been in the class for several years, although one member joined on one of the Sundays when we were sharing spiritual family trees. Every few months we choose what we'll study for the next few months. Sometimes it's part of the Bible. Sometimes it's a book one of us has especially liked. Sometimes it's a series from our denomination's publishing house. Sometimes it's material we put together ourselves, on a topic we're currently interested in.

One Sunday Larry suggested that we share spiritual family trees. He's a United Methodist clergyman who for the past seven years had been a chaplain and teacher at a local hospital and medical school. He had used genograms to build community and explore the influences on spiritual growth. He thought our class might find the process interesting, probably spending two or three Sundays on it. Little did we know!

## Larry's Spiritual Family Tree

When the time for sharing arrived, Larry explained the process and presented his own spiritual family tree *(see figure 1 on page 6 )*. We were intrigued. We had thought we knew him fairly well, but we learned all sorts of new things about him. Here's what he told us.

I grew up primarily in a rural part of the United States. My parents grew up on adjoining farms and were very active in their local Church of Christ, an independent congregation. My paternal grandmother's church considered her their official pray-er because she prayed such

4

eloquent public prayers. After she and her family and church members had considered that as her main spiritual gift and calling for years, however, a new pastor came. He told her that women weren't supposed to hold leadership roles in the church. He forbade her from praying publicly anymore. She was crushed. Her experience is one of the main reasons I now feel strongly about the need for women church leaders and also the need to avoid using all-masculine language that at best makes women seem inferior and at worst makes them virtually invisible.

With the help of the GI Bill, my parents left the farm and my father received his bachelor's degree in agriculture. He managed a feed and farm supply store his whole career. In a change from their Church of Christ roots, my parents became Methodist before I was born. This was mainly because when my father had serious surgery, the only pastor who visited him during his convalescence was a Methodist minister. So when I was growing up I often heard family members talk about how important it is to visit the sick.

I also heard a lot about the importance of being part of the church, and I experienced it constantly. My family went regularly to all the activities of the local Methodist church. We were there for youth groups, for regular worship, and for special services. So from as early as I can remember, I got the message that living out our faith was important.

The civil rights movement influenced my family a lot. Our schools were integrated when I was in elementary school. We watched Martin Luther King, Jr.'s "I Have a Dream" speech together as a family. In our conversations about current events I learned that my parents' great-great-grandparents fought for the North in the Civil War because they wanted the slaves freed. And that was why they were still in the Republican party—Lincoln's party. We talked about equality and rights for all. I remember this turbulent time as drawing our family together and confirming our spiritual beliefs about the importance of promoting justice and mercy for everyone.

In college, I majored in forestry, preparing to be a forest ranger. But the Vietnam War and the demonstrations against the war were constantly in the news. My family and friends talked a lot about what

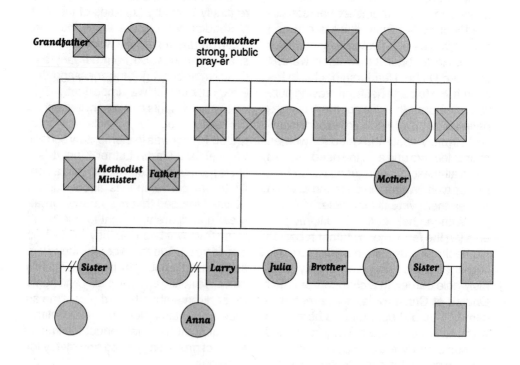

**Figure 1. Larry's Genogram**

these events meant. I began thinking that a forest ranger wasn't what I needed to be. Ministry and social service entered my thoughts as we discussed what it meant to be faithful during those difficult times.

After graduation I spent two years in the Peace Corps. When I came home, I went to seminary and became an ordained minister. After seminary I entered a training program to become a chaplain and a chaplain educator. I had been in the program for two years before it occurred to me that my father, when he was sick, was visited by a Methodist minister. I've always wondered if that part of my family history influenced my desire to become a chaplain.

While sharing my spiritual family tree here in our Sunday School class I've remembered a gift given to me by one of our class members. One Sunday during the dark time several years ago when I was going through a divorce and getting ready to move to a new state and a new job, one of our class members encouraged me. Steve* pointed out to me, "You have Easter with you all the time, in your name—Easterling. It can be your constant

reminder of the resurrection and new life that's always available to you."

*Throughout this book, names and other identifying features have been changed to preserve confidentiality, for all quoted tree-sharers except Barbara and Larry.*

## Barbara's Spiritual Family Tree

By the time Larry finished sharing his spiritual family tree, all of us who had heard it were excited about having other class members share theirs. The next Sunday Barbara presented hers *(see figure 2).*

In my family when I was growing up, we were very active in the Methodist church but we never talked about religious beliefs or social or political issues. We never discussed the pros and cons of generally accepted customs or current proval of traditions and conventions was unthinkable. To me, even questioning

7

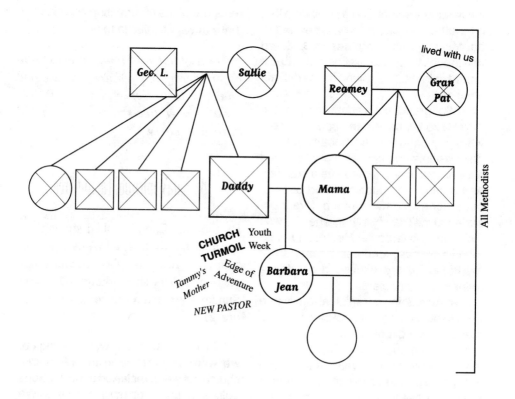

**Figure 2. Barbara's Genogram**

8

such things seemed unthinkable.

We didn't pray openly, either. My father (or my mother, when he was absent) always said "the blessing"—a short, rote prayer—at the beginning of family meals, but if my parents prayed spontaneously or read the Bible, it must have been in private, because I wasn't aware of it. Although I've done a lot of looking at my own life and at the church on my own in recent years, only now, in telling this, am I beginning to realize how this kind of privacy keeps children from learning what being a Christian really means.

The only exception I remember was during my high school or college years, when I was vaguely aware of my father's efforts (and my mother's disapproval of them), to combat what he saw as dangerous liberal trends in the church. In telling this, I see how similar my present efforts to change the church are to his, although what I think needs changing is the opposite of what disturbed him.

I grew up thinking that all women were supposed to be full-time wives and mothers, no matter what their talents and interests were. That's the only pattern I saw when I looked at my family, friends, and the other members of our churches. So after graduating from college and working as a mathematician for a few years, when I married I quit my job and settled into the role that I thought was the only role for a woman.

During all those years I got the impression that being a Christian merely meant participating fully in the institutional church, being "nice," and conforming to religious and social traditions. Seeking, getting, and following current personal guidance from God never occurred to me. Neither did working to promote justice in the church or the world by opposing customs like racial segregation and keeping women subservient, customs that apparently were accepted without question by everyone I knew.

I certainly never thought of God calling me to do anything. As a lifelong churchgoer, I had of course heard about people who were called by God, but the ones in the Bible were radical prophets (and apparently all men) like Jeremiah, or unique leaders like Moses and Paul and the gospel writers. Later ones were unique, radical, disruptive people too. They weren't anything like anyone I knew.

My experience had made me assume that in more recent times God called people only to be pastors (who were all men), missionaries (to grim places like Outer Mongolia), or directors of religious education (unmarried women who wore dark crepe dresses, sensible shoes, no makeup, and sweetly pious facial expressions). I felt sure none of those roles were for me.

A few widely scattered exceptions to the church routine came during those years. The most notable was a young guest pastor who led an annual Youth Week at my church. His sermon based on the "Here am I, send me" scripture from the book of Isaiah gave me a glimpse of an aspect of Christianity I'd never previously seen. His dynamic personality and powerful sermons during dramatic worship services were a surprising and welcome contrast to all that I had seen in routine Sunday School classes, worship services, and youth activities. He made me realize that being a Christian could mean experiencing God's presence. He made me aware that being a Christian meant being committed to bold

action. I saw for the first time that being a Christian didn't mean the lukewarm, robot-like participation I'd previously known. Nor did it mean having a bland, colorless appearance and personality like most of the church leaders I'd seen. But because none of this matched anything I knew, I banished it from my mind for many years. Years later, when as a young mother I was regularly teaching second-grade Sunday School, I was shocked to find myself suddenly in position to support a child in my class when her mother unexpectedly died. I felt God had somehow put me in this position, but this experience, too, was so unlike anything else I'd ever known that I banished it from my awareness for years. I didn't know what else to do with it.

At midlife, to my great surprise, my view of myself and of the church started changing. I had finished the daily mothering duties and the church and community volunteer jobs that had kept me busy for the previous 20 years or so, and I couldn't see anything to replace them. I couldn't see anything interesting or challenging when I looked ahead, and that was very discouraging. As a result I began questioning things I'd never thought of questioning before, or had at least never dared to question openly. I began seeing the injustice in the pattern that required women to stay in the background and forget about pursuing their main interests and using their main abilities. Turmoil in my local church made me start thinking about what the church's real purpose was, and realizing that a lot of churches' usual activities didn't seem likely to accomplish it.

Following a lifelong habit of reading, I began looking for answers in books. My reading reminded me of how starved I was for the intellectual stimulation I'd been away from for so many years, and for interaction with people who were thinking, reading, talking, and maybe even doing something about what I was only reading and thinking about.

After reading and reflecting alone for a while, I finally felt starved enough to get out and look for the kindred spirits and mental activity I longed for. To my surprise, the new pastor of my church asked me about my interests and revealed that he read and thought about the same kinds of things I was reading and thinking about. No previous pastor had ever done that.

Even more surprising, when I began looking for college courses to give me the intellectual stimulation I wanted, I found that seminaries offered the combination of subjects I wanted. I was so delighted with the first course I took at a seminary that I kept commuting to that seminary for three years to get a master's degree. I found still more kindred spirits in a spiritual-formation program that included laity and clergy from all over the United States. I took part in it while attending seminary.

While I was participating in those two life-changing programs I started journaling for personal reflection and prayer. That eventually led to writing for publication, and then to writing and publishing a monthly newsletter about the need for spiritual renewal in mainline churches. My newsletter has led to public-speaking opportunities and to welcome contact with even more kindred spirits.

Hearing Barbara's story was an eye-opener for many class members who knew of her writing and speaking but hadn't known how they differed from the quiet, unquestioning conformity that had previously been her habit. From her story class members saw that "spiritual ancestors" aren't always family members, or even people we know personally. Barbara's most influential spiritual ancestors were the authors whose writings she read, and certain pastors and church members whom she found to be kindred spirits.

## Becoming a Community

The next Sunday Gary presented his spiritual family tree to the class. By then several other class members were looking forward to doing theirs. By then, too, Fran had joined the class. She found our presentations an ideal way to get to know the rest of us. The Sunday after she joined, she did hers, which let us get to

know her quickly. Newcomers to a long-established class like ours often feel like outsiders, but by sharing spiritual family trees, it's easy to become instant insiders.

The two or three Sundays that we had originally thought our spiritual family tree series would fill kept growing. By the end of each Sunday's session another class member was counting on being the next Sunday's presenter.

For the first few weeks Steve kept saying, "I wouldn't want to tell all that about my life." Then one Sunday morning he suddenly said, "Maybe I'll do mine sometime. I'm thinking about it." A week or two later he said, "I'll do mine next Sunday."

Eventually every class member took a turn. Although some members' presentations took only a few minutes, most filled a full class session. Three months after we began sharing spiritual family trees, we finally ended the series with a wrap-up session. In looking at what the experience had meant to us, we saw benefits that had come to each of us and to our class as a whole. We saw the similarity to earlier Christians' use of sharing, such as the Methodist "class meetings" instituted by John Wesley. We saw common features in our spiritual family trees, despite their surface differences. We saw important lessons in these common features, for the church, for families, and for individual Christians who want to grow spiritually. And we saw that by getting to know each other better we had come to care more about each other. We had become a real community.

We've now seen other groups receive similar benefits from sharing spiritual family trees. That's why we want to share our experience with you and invite you to share spiritual family trees in the groups you belong to.

## Looking Deeper

- What aspects of your own spiritual history have Larry's and Barbara's accounts brought to mind?

- What "spiritual ancestors" have been most influential for you?

- Have you ever shared your spiritual history with anyone as fully as Larry and Barbara have shared theirs here?

- Would you welcome the opportunity to share your story with someone, or does the thought of doing so make you uneasy?

- With whom would you find it hardest to share your spiritual history? Your spouse? Your parents? Your children? A close friend? Your religious group? A stranger? Your congregation, if you're a pastor? Which of these would be easiest? What makes the difference?

13

# CHAPTER 2

# Learning about Genograms

To help you decide whether to accept our invitation to draw and share your spiritual family tree, or to use spiritual family trees in a religious group you lead, you may want to know a little more about genograms.

Using them for identifying religious roots is relatively recent. Genograms were originally created for other purposes. Then people began realizing that they were helpful for seeing how our religious and spiritual backgrounds influence us.

For quite a few years some doctors have used genograms for gathering medical history. Looking at certain diseases or deformities within several generations of a family helps both doctors and their patients see possible causes of these ailments. This, of course, helps researchers on their quest for cures.

Therapists have used genograms for years. Seeing behavioral patterns that recur in several generations of a family, and seeing how the family functions as a system in which all members influence each other, helps psychotherapists suggest changes to break the cycle. If you'd like to know more about how therapists use genograms, we suggest *Genograms*, by Monica McGoldrick, Randy Gerson, and Sylvia Shellenberger.[1]

Unfortunately, therapists often fail to look at the spiritual and religious aspects of clients' lives and families. According to Marsha Wiggins Frame, a clergy-woman and professor of counseling psychology, "Despite the fact that most Americans report that they believe in God and 75% call themselves religious, many marriage and family therapists feel challenged to deal with clients' religious/ spiritual beliefs." Lack of training in this area, she believes, is the cause—a cause that needs remedying. "Despite some therapists' discomfort in working with religious or spiritual issues," Frame observes, "this aspect of clients' lives is a dimension that affects the way they function."

Frame finds the genogram an ideal tool for looking at that aspect of life. "The spiritual genogram enables clients to gain a new perspective on ways in which their religious/spiritual heritage continues to affect their current beliefs and practices." In fact, she believes that therapists are ethically obligated to learn how to address their clients' religious and spiritual concerns.[2]

Religious and business leaders are also starting to see the importance of religious and spiritual beliefs. After noticing the similarities between the way organizations and families function, these leaders have realized that looking at how the parts of a group affect each other is often more helpful than looking at the parts separately.

Families, corporations, and religious communities—all kinds of systems— function like a physical body. Whatever one part does affects the other parts. If your foot gets hurt and you start limping, your back muscles soon start hurting because you're walking differently to protect your sore foot. Treating your backache isn't likely to help as long as you're still limping.

It's a lot like a manufacturing business. If a hailstorm puts several delivery trucks out of service, for example, the resulting backlog in manufacturing will soon keep production workers from making products, which will result in a deluge of calls from angry customers, which will have to be handled by office staff, and so on. None of these departments experiences the problem alone. The whole system is affected.

In thinking through the part-whole relationship, two quite different paths—therapy and organizational management—have in a sense arrived at the same spot. The usefulness of genograms and other family-systems tools has become apparent. In religious groups we can now see that when members examine and share their spiritual histories, they not only grow spiritually as individuals but also enjoy an increased sense of community. Religious groups urgently need this result.

As a leader or other member of a religious group, then, you may want to become more familiar with genograms and some ways of using them.

## Medical Uses

You probably are familiar with physicians taking a family history as part of a physical. During your first appointment with a new physician, even before she examines you she's likely to ask you about family illnesses that may relate to your long-term care. Questions about disease processes, causes of death, and other medical procedures help the physician place you in the context of your family medical history.

If you've ever peeked at your medical chart, you may have seen a genogram, which looks like a family tree. Figure 3 (page 18) shows what one might look like.

Figure 4 (page 19) shows what the symbols in a genogram represent. Usually the squares represent males in the family and the circles represent females. (We'll avoid mentioning what this might imply about males being "square.")

The "charting" shown in figure 3 is a shorthand version of what patients tell a physician in response to questions about their health and their family medical history. If figure 1 represented your medical history and you were the patient represented in the lower left-hand section

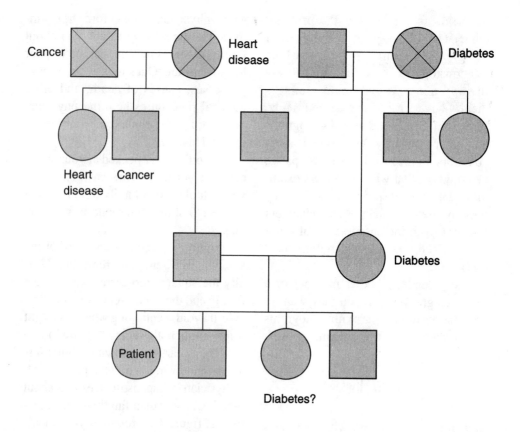

**Figure 3. Medical history sample genogram**

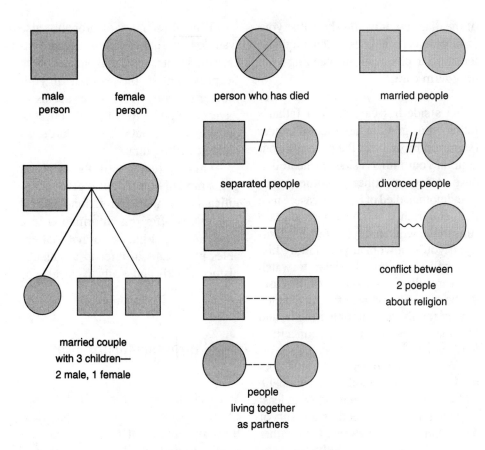

male person

female person

person who has died

married people

separated people

divorced people

married couple with 3 children— 2 male, 1 female

people living together as partners

conflict between 2 poeple about religion

**Figure 4. Explanation of symbols**

19

of the diagram, it would show that your family has certain illnesses that might interest your physician in planning your long-term care.

For instance, your uncle on your father's side has cancer. Your father's father, your grandfather, died of cancer (signified by an X in the square). Your aunt on your father's side has heart disease and your father's mother, your grandmother, died of heart disease. Since the genogram shows that heart disease runs in the women in your father's family, if you're a woman your family history will alert your physician to watch you carefully for signs of heart disease. At the same time, cancer runs in the men in your family, on your father's side, and this may show a cause for concern if you're male.

As for your mother's side, your doctor sees that your mother is a diabetic and your maternal grandmother, at least to your knowledge, died as a result of her diabetes. Your maternal grandfather is 80 and apparently healthy. Perhaps you will inherit some of that longevity.

Your physician will probably also want to know about your eating and exercising habits, since diabetes seems to be prevalent in the women of your mother's family. Your sister seems to have some problem with early onset of diabetes as well, but you're not sure she's diabetic at this point.

This is just a simple medical genogram, of course, but it gives a significant amount of information. Medical genograms offer this information in a condensed, at-a-glance format that enables physicians to refer to a patient's history quickly and easily. It can also be updated conveniently.

# Psychotherapeutic Uses

What about using genograms in psychotherapy? The modern psychotherapy movement began in earnest with Sigmund Freud's investigation of the life of the mind. He believed that early involvement with our primary caregiver, usually the mother, shapes our personhood. His therapy, then, focused on revealing patients' inner conflicts about their primary caretakers. In Freud's method, one therapist and one patient worked together to heal the patient. No other family members needed to be present, because they would have little or nothing to contribute. Obviously this is an oversimplified description of Freud's work, but it provides a basic picture of his methods.

Over the last hundred years many other schools of therapy have arisen, some growing out of Freud's methods and others opposing them. One that arose in opposition to Freud's work is family systems therapy. Murray Bowen, M.D., from Georgetown Medical School, originated one of the most prominent forms of this therapy. Family systems therapy recognizes that, in contrast to what Freud thought, family is a complex, dynamic force in people's lives and thus a major influence therapists need to consider.

Family systems theorists believe that many of the conflicts and stresses Freud believed lived inside the patient reside instead within the relational dynamics of the immediate, extended, and multigenerational family. Because a family systems therapist can observe the pertinent family relationships in the here and now, in the therapist's office, family systems theorists believe that by observing these relational dynamics and intervening in constructive ways, therapists can help families function better.

The family systems movement includes many different schools of thought. In almost all forms of family systems theory, however, five basic concepts appear. They are (1) identified patient, (2) homeostasis, (3) differentiation of self, (4) emotional triangles, and (5) intergenerational repetition.

## Identified Patient: Who Is the Patient?

Unlike Freud, family systems theorists view the person who comes for therapy, the "identified patient," as the carrier of family symptoms, but they view the whole family as the real patient. For this reason, some therapists will work only with the entire family, while others will work with whichever family members are willing and able to participate in therapy.

Rather than see a mechanistic cause and effect—one person merely doing things to another—family systems therapy sees the whole family system as interrelated. Mother influences child, as child influences mother, as mother influences father, as father influences child, and so on. Each person in the system has an effect on and is affected by all the others. In this sense family systems therapists see their model as more dynamic, more complicated, more biological, and more wholistic.

## Homeostasis: Balance at All Costs?

In the family system "homeostasis" refers to the balance between the emotional structure and the relational patterns that have developed over time. The family's emotional and relational "tone" becomes familiar and thus comfortable even if it is harmful. When a family member tries to change his or her behavior, this disrupts the emotional and relational balance. The family therefore exerts pressure on that person to return to the old behavior. If the person "gets back into line," the old homeostasis is preserved. If the person persists in the new behavior, a new homeostasis will eventually emerge and will be as difficult to change as the old homeostasis was.

For example, adolescence is difficult for the whole family because the adolescent is trying on new and often independent behavior. A new teenage driver causes family anxiety partly because adding a driver disrupts the order of the family—it disrupts the family's homeostasis.

Other changes make family members uncomfortable, too. If the women of the family tend to be shy and docile, seen but not heard, it creates great turmoil when Mom begins to speak her mind. Dad and other family members may pressure her to return to her old self, behaving the way that was comfortable for the rest of the family. Phrases such as "What's come over you?" or "You're not yourself anymore" point to the family's desire to return to the old homeostasis.

## Differentiation of Self: Who Is Cold?

Another concept basic to family systems theory is "differentiation of self." Here the individual's goal is to differentiate from the other members of the family. An oversimplified but still useful example of failure to differentiate is the story of a parent and child riding in a car together. The parent becomes cold and says to the child, "Put your coat on."

A more complex example of differentiation in families is parents expecting their children to feel the same way as the parents, about other people, events, issues, or beliefs. In some families, for instance, being a Republican (or a Democrat) is very important to the family's identity. If a child chooses to be otherwise, great anxiety arises. A parent may say to the child, "This family has always been Republican. I can't believe you could be a Democrat! How could we have failed so miserably? What will Aunt Alice (the senator) say when she hears this?" Persisting in being something else would require a great deal of energy from the child and would cause some discomfort, both to the child and to the rest of the family, so the child relents and steps back into line, especially after a heart-to-heart talk with Aunt Alice.

In contrast, holding different viewpoints is permissible in healthy, functioning families. In such a family the child would say something like, "I see your point, Dad, but I see it this way," and father and child would agree to disagree.

Dad would not try to bring the "errant" child back into line.

The goal of differentiation is being in relationship with others rather than emotionally cutting them off or giving in to them. Achieving this goal requires having a clear understanding of yourself and having the ability to be comfortable with the other's point of view even when it differs from your own.

## Emotional Triangles: Whose Conflict Is This?

Identifying "emotional triangles" is another key feature of family systems theory. Bowen, like other family systems theorists, believed that the most stable dynamic of relationships plays itself out in a set of three people. This could be father/mother/child, father/mother/grandmother, or any other set of three family members.

One common emotional triangle is seen when parents bring a child to therapy. They present the child as emotionally sick. As long as the child accepts this role in the family there is some sense of balance. Quite often, however, the parents are focusing on the child's "problem" in order to avoid acknowledging the tension in their own relationship. They ignore the parental relationship and "triangle" the child into it in order to avoid that tension.

We can see a national emotional triangle in the tension between Republicans and Democrats these days. In earlier years, when the Soviet Union was the third party in the triangle, Republicans and Democrats could work together on common problems, for the good of the nation. But as soon as the Soviet Union disintegrated, the long-standing tensions between Republicans and Democrats resurfaced and could no longer be ignored.

## Intergenerational Repetition: Like Parent, Like Child?

The last of the five key features of family systems theory, "intergenerational repetition," connects directly to spiritual family trees. Families tend to repeat behavioral patterns and feelings from one generation to the next, especially if these patterns go unexamined. Certain common phrases show our awareness of this: "He didn't fall far from the tree" and "Like mother, like daughter." A well-known biblical family, Joseph's family, described in the book of Genesis in the Hebrew scriptures, illustrates this aspect of family systems (*see fig. 5 on page 26*).

Tension and treachery between members of Joseph's family run through several generations. Joseph's great-grandfather, Abraham, fearing that King Abimelech might kill him, tricks Abimelech into believing that Abraham's wife, Sarah, is Abraham's sister. Joseph's grandfather, Laban, tricks Jacob, Joseph's father, into marrying Laban's daughter Leah when Jacob believes he is marrying Rachel, her sister. Jacob then tricks Laban out of the best sheep and goats after working for Laban for many years. Jacob and his mother, Rebecca, conspire to trick Rebecca's husband, Isaac, into blessing Jacob, thereby denying Jacob's brother Esau his natural birthright. Through treachery Joseph's brothers sell Joseph into slavery. They falsely tell their father, Jacob, that Joseph is dead, and Jacob believes them when they show him Joseph's bloody cloak.

The deception that began with Abraham and Sarah repeats itself throughout the generations. Jacob and Rebecca trick Isaac. Laban tricks Jacob. Jacob tricks Laban. And Joseph's brothers trick Jacob, claiming that Joseph was killed by a wild animal. Joseph even repeats the pattern. He tricks his brothers by placing a gold cup in Benjamin's bag, making them fear that Benjamin's life was in danger because he had stolen the cup.

Joseph and his family members wouldn't have gone to a therapist, of course, but the generational repetition of trickery and deception in his family is the

25

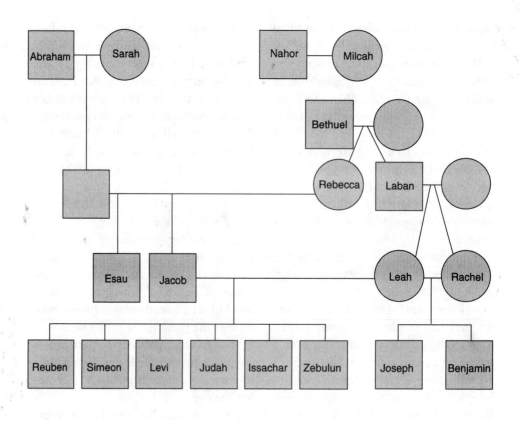

**Figure 5. Joseph's genogram**

kind of repetitive dynamics that family therapists examine. The ultimate goal of family systems therapy is to help families discover such repetitions and structure their lives differently in order to change their destructive patterns. Likewise, discovering such patterns in our religious backgrounds can help those of us who want our religious groups to be the true communities God calls them to be.

## Spiritual Uses

Until very recently most psychologists and psychiatrists did not address religious or spiritual issues. Freud felt that such issues were powerful but illusory and thus were impediments to mental health. He believed that when therapy was finished, religious beliefs would be unnecessary. Family systems therapists have continued this tradition, often regarding religion or spirituality as too volatile to address in therapy, or at the very least feeling unprepared to deal with the issue. By including spiritual issues when we look at family systems, however, we expand our understanding of families and the other groups we belong to.

Treachery and deceit are clearly present in Joseph's family, but so is another prominent theme that we can't ignore if we want a true picture of the family: great faith in a merciful God. Abraham and Sarah left their homeland trusting that God was calling them to something new. Abraham and Sarah trusted God's promise to make from them a great people. Abraham, because of his faith in God, was ready to sacrifice Isaac, the hope and dream of that great people. Because of a merciful and faithful God, Isaac was spared and the Judeo-Christian world knows Abraham and Sarah as people of great faith.

Joseph's father, Jacob, wrestled with God's angel at the river Jabok and was blessed. He and Esau, who demonstrated great forgiveness, were reconciled, apparently because they grew in faith as they grew in years. Joseph's own faith in God sustains him while in prison in

Egypt and in his leadership of the Egyptian kingdom. Ultimately Joseph shows mercy toward his treacherous brothers because of his maturing faith in the God of Abraham and Sarah, Isaac and Rebecca, and Jacob and Rachel.

Throughout the Bible you can see other examples of religious attitudes and beliefs, both helpful and harmful, recurring through several generations. In the second letter to Timothy, for example: "I am reminded of your sincere faith that lived first in your grandmother Lois and your mother Eunice and now, I am sure, lives in you" (2 Timothy 1:5).

Later Christian history includes examples, too. Susannah Wesley, the mother of John and Charles Wesley, who began the Methodist movement, played a giant role in the religious education of her children. And what about Augustine, the fourth-century Christian leader whose influence continued for centuries? His non-Christian father steered him toward an interest in philosophy, and he depended to a great extent on the piety of his Christian mother.

Spirituality and religious practice play vital roles in individuals' lives, and spirituality and religion can help or harm their mental health. Looking at our spiritual family trees is therefore a useful tool in nourishing that health. That's not the only way spiritual family trees can help us, however. They also increase our ability to function in healthy ways in the groups we're part of, including religious groups.

"Families are not groups and groups are not families," Daniel C. DeArment, a teacher of pastoral care, rightly observes.[3] As DeArment and other observers point out, however, families and other groups function similarly. Family systems theory has thrown light on these similarities in recent years. If this subject is new to you and you'd like to read more about how religious groups operate like families, and how recognizing the similarities can help religious leaders to lead more effectively, we suggest *Generation to Generation*, by Rabbi Edwin H. Friedman.[4]

When we are involved in building a faith community, we draw on our experience of faith. When we enter religious groups, however, just as when we enter groups in educational, social, or work settings, we also bring our understanding of what being in a group means. And that understanding, stated or unstated, known or unknown, comes mostly from our experience of family life. Therefore if in our religious groups we don't explore how members expect groups to function, our effectiveness as leaders and participants suffers.

Because building an intimate and nurturing faith community depends on becoming aware of what each member expects from group life, sharing spiritual family trees serves several purposes:

- It helps us identify the important people of faith in our families.

- It helps us identify the valued spiritual covenants, concepts, and thoughts that have been part of our experience.

- It helps us identify the particular faith tradition that has influenced us most.

In building a community of faith we need these identifications for two reasons. First, we need to see more clearly where we have come from in our faith journey. Second, when we become more aware of our own beliefs and attitudes and where some of them came from, we become more open to discovering the valuable contributions—sacred contributions, in fact—of other members of the group. Sharing spiritual family trees helps group participants see how they can learn from each other through becoming aware of how their different backgrounds have influenced their present views and beliefs.

The purpose of building a community of faith, then, is to nourish the spiritual journey of each person and of the group as a whole. By sharing spiritual family trees we build on the wealth of others' experiences. Sharing our spiritual family trees also binds us with

29

persons and groups of the past who have struggled to be faithful, just as we and other group members are struggling. Discovering others' journeys will thus enrich the faith journey we are making together.

In the next chapter we'll look at how sharing spiritual family trees can help a group become the kind of community that functions effectively and makes people want to be part of it.

## Looking Deeper

- How have your religious beliefs influenced the way you function in your daily life?

- How has your family or religious group been influenced when a member changed his or her behavior? How did others respond? Was the group helped or hurt in the long run? How might a different response have been more helpful, for the group or the member or both?

- If you aren't in the tradition from which Barbara's and Larry's examples come, how have your tradition's leaders been influenced by their families?

- How have you benefited from becoming aware of someone's religious or cultural background, especially if it was different from yours?

# CHAPTER 3

# Building Community

Now that we've reviewed some of the history of genograms and the ways therapists have used them, let's look at how they can be useful in religious groups. Members of these groups don't come for therapy; they come for community. Genograms, when used as a part of sharing spiritual family trees, can help to build this community. Before we go into detail about how to use genograms in community building, however, we will look at how two church members—one a layman and the other a pastor—shared spiritual family trees in their groups and saw exciting results.

## Sharing Faith Stories: Two Examples

### Sharing on Short Notice

Greg, a Christian layman, discovered that using the spiritual family tree format lets us share our personal experiences more fully than does ordinary conversation or typical group sharing. When we tell our stories in typical group sessions or in ordinary conversation, he observes, "things come out only in bits and pieces."

Greg presented his spiritual family tree when the main speaker cancelled and Greg was enlisted to fill in at a spiritual-growth program reunion. Even though he had little advance notice, by thinking quickly about his "bits and pieces" and then presenting them in spiritual family tree format, Greg was able to describe his spiritual journey more clearly, more concisely, and more completely than he otherwise could have. He also found that sharing in this way was fun, and it made him feel more a part of the group.

At the end of his presentation many group members complimented and thanked Greg. They found that hearing his story in the spiritual family tree format helped them know him better and feel closer to him. His presentation, they told him, also shed new light on their own spiritual journeys.

Because of this experience Greg is now planning to use the spiritual family tree format in his neighborhood Bible study group. He expects that sharing spiritual family trees will help group members know each other better and become closer. As he did at the beginning of his reunion presentation, Greg plans to ask group members to think about their own spiritual journeys as they hear about his and those of other members.

## Sharing in Adult Classes

Alice, a pastor at a rural church, also found sharing spiritual family trees helpful. It increased not only her own personal spiritual growth but also her effectiveness in her job. In addition, she found that this kind of sharing promoted closeness among members of her church.

Alice taught her church's only adult class. She introduced spiritual family trees to the small class shortly after the class formed. Its members didn't know each other well, and although their ages varied widely, most of the class members were newer and younger than the congregation's other members.

Alice shared her own spiritual family tree first. She wasn't optimistic about any other class members' volunteering to share theirs, but she was pleasantly surprised. Most members shared their trees, and the sharing continued for two months. Alice says the project created more enthusiasm than anything else the class had ever done.

This experience helped her as pastor, helped the class members individually and as a group, and helped the church. Because Alice shared her spiritual journey with class members, they came to trust her more than they previously had. They began seeing her as one of them, rather than merely the latest new pastor sent to their church.

Class members' presentations helped Alice know them better, too. She came to understand some of the reasons for attitudes, beliefs, and behavior she'd previously found hard to cope with. Hearing about one member's upbringing in the rural South, for example, gave her insight into his disturbing tendency to make racist comments.

Some members, Alice found, knew little about their parents' and grandparents'

church participation. Many of their parents and grandparents had been in different church denominations, and several hadn't been churchgoers. This was quite different from Alice's family experience, and explained members' apathetic or even negative attitudes toward the church. Hearing class members' spiritual family trees therefore enabled Alice to become a more sympathetic and effective pastor.

For most members, Alice found, at least one experience had strongly influenced their beliefs and views. For some it was an apparently miraculous recovery from a serious illness. For others it was a painful job change or the death of a loved one. As members recalled and described these experiences, Alice felt as though she was seeing lightbulbs go on over the heads of the presenters as well as the listeners. In response to their fellow members' presentations, many commented, "I can see now why you feel the way you do." Sharing spiritual family trees brought them closer and helped them understand each other better.

To Alice's surprise, after class members started sharing spiritual family trees she began to see them talk with each other outside of class, sharing their current experiences and feelings and asking about each other's well-being. A real sense of intimacy developed. Members' commitment to the church increased, too. They began talking to Alice and to each other about improvements to the church building and about new ministries the congregation might start in the local community.

Perhaps most important, in Alice's view, was the regard class members showed for each other during the tree sharing. All were treated as if their stories were interesting and important. "No one was ignored or discounted," she says. "There was a sacredness about it, a sanctity that was very clear." In her future pastorates Alice definitely plans to use spiritual family tree sharing to build familiarity and a sense of community between members.

For several years we have seen that need for intimacy and community, and we have tried to help the church respond to it. Larry has been involved in educating clergy to provide competent and compassionate pastoral care not only to church members but also to the surrounding community. Barbara has written extensively on reenergizing the local church, especially by urging its lay members to take more active roles in its ministries. Now, however, we both see that sharing spiritual family trees is a valuable way for both the clergy and the laity to help build their faith communities into the strong centers of love and justice that God calls them to be.

# Sharing Stories: A Brief History

Before we look further at how religious groups can share spiritual family trees, let's briefly explore how other ways of sharing personal faith stories have played important roles in the church. We'll also look at how the resemblance between religious organizations and family groups has influenced pastoral care in recent years.

Using the family tree format for sharing faith stories in religious groups is relatively new, but sharing these stories isn't new at all. Throughout human history both religious and secular groups have recognized the value of sharing personal stories in group building. Having a strong faith community was especially important at the beginning of many faith traditions. Indeed, some of these traditions flourished more at their beginning than they do now. We can't attribute their decline to any one cause, of course, but the decreased emphasis on meeting in small groups and sharing personal faith stories may be a contributing factor.

The earliest Christians gathered regularly in small groups, often in members' homes, for support, prayer, and in many cases personal safety. Later, during the Reformation, small groups led by Martin Luther drew strength from each other when they gathered to escape religious persecution. In the beginning of the Wesleyan movement—whose successor, the United Methodist Church, we both belong to—small groups were also vital for its growth and sustenance. While in college at Oxford, John Wesley and his brother Charles, the founders of Methodism, belonged to a small group known as the Holy Club. Its members met regularly to pray and to study the scriptures. Holy Club members were so devoted to their group and their praying and studying that they were derisively called "Methodists" because of their methodical meetings and their individual use of strict spiritual disciplines.

It is interesting to note that this use of small group support for faith development did not spring full-grown from either John or Charles Wesley. Throughout their early years their mother, Susanna, led prayer meetings in the home and on occasion read sermons and led

35

discussions about "acts of devotion." Susanna Wesley's devotional life and her belief that small group prayer and study helped Christians live out their faith must have had a strong impact on both John and Charles. Because in their childhood home they had seen the benefits of small-group support and personal spiritual disciplines, throughout their later lives they joined groups that provided or created groups to provide such benefits.

The "class meetings" and "bands" that were part of early Methodism are largely credited with the spread of Methodism throughout England and the United States. Local leaders gathered these groups and focused on their members' relationship with God, praying, and studying scriptures. Hearing accounts of members' previous and current religious experience was an important part of each group meeting. For their members, these groups provided support, spiritual sustenance, and in some cases even physical safety from the larger community of unsympathetic Anglicans

in England or residents of early America's wilderness.

Many observers believe that the bands and societies were the main reason for the growth of the early Methodist church. "If ever the society or local church became too unwieldy," explains Wesley scholar Frederick A. Norwood, "at least in the small class meeting intimate community could be maintained."[1] Around the middle of the nineteenth century, class meetings began to decline as itinerant ministers began settling as part of local church congregations instead of traveling continually. When the pastor came only once a month or so, a lay class leader had to organize the church and take responsibility for promoting the spiritual health of the church and its members. "But when the preacher settled down in a parsonage as a stationed pastor, the class leader (and along with him the local preacher and exhorter) became, at least so it seemed, an unnecessary wheel," Norwood writes. "Inadvertently, because of the settling down of the traveling preacher, Methodism lost one of its strongest supports, the active *ministerial* participation of the lay people."[2]

Within today's United Methodist Church we find Bishop James R. King, Jr., along with many other leaders, calling United Methodists back to their roots. "I am proposing that we return to our Christian roots and our biblical and Wesleyan heritage," King writes. "Can you see five to eight persons (or whatever the number) meeting weekly for prayer, study, sharing and support?"[3]

We have focused on the United Methodist Church's history because it happens to be our faith tradition, but we encourage you to examine your own faith community's history. Notice how sharing faith stories or using other ways of building faith in small groups may have helped to establish and maintain your faith tradition.

# Modern Pastoral Care

Along with changing social conditions, the modern Protestant pastoral care movement has further hastened the demise of churches' earlier focus on small groups and the telling of personal stories at group gatherings. For the most part, modern liberal Protestant pastoral care has used the psychotherapeutic models generated by Freud and his followers. Freud's psychoanalytic movement focused on the health of the individual in the midst of a supposedly hostile society. The pastoral care movement has also tended to focus on helping individuals to mature so that they can function more effectively even when surrounded by a society that seems hostile, as a non-Christian society often does to Christians.

A more recent movement that has advocated focusing pastoral care on the individual's growth and maturation process is Clinical Pastoral Education (CPE), led by clergy and physicians. Begun in 1925, mainly in hospitals, CPE trains pastors to be hospital chaplains. This movement makes extensive use of "verbatims," long narratives of pastoral visits, centered on the one-on-one relationship between the patient and the pastor serving as a hospital chaplain.

CPE training gives much attention to the pastor's personal therapeutic issues. For example, if a pastor hasn't resolved issues related to the death of a child, spouse, parent, or someone else close to him, he won't be able to give needed help to anyone else who is experiencing a similar loss. Or if a pastor always needs to feel like an authority to feel good about herself, when she's ministering to a hospital patient she'll tend to do all the talking instead of letting the patient talk. Such therapeutic issues, according to CPE training, can inhibit the pastor from being fully present with the patient in the patient's journey toward mental health. The CPE movement has thus paralleled other recent trends in psychology by emphasizing individual growth rather than an individual's role as a member of a group.

Only in the last ten years has pastoral care reembraced the group model of personal growth. Family systems theory and social systems theory have also influenced the pastoral care movement's recent return to an emphasis on family and group dynamics.

An especially important leader in opening the discussion of a broader understanding of pastoral care has been John Patton. For him, pastoral care includes more than the understanding of a pastor's care for a parishioner, which is basically a one-on-one relationship. Patton sees pastoral care also as "a ministry of the Christian community that takes place through remembering God's action for us, remembering who we are as God's own people, and hearing and remembering those to whom we minister."[4]

Charles Gerkin, another leader in the pastoral care movement, expands on Patton's perspective. "Ministry of the church," according to Gerkin, involves not only "care of the identifying Christian tradition, the contemporary community of

Christians, and the particular needs of the individuals within the community" but also, and always, "giving attention to the issues and concerns of the contemporary cultural context."[5]

Both Patton and Gerkin remind us that, in addition to the pastor's one-on-one pastoral care or the therapist's individual counseling, the church family also can play a major role in an individual's nurture and growth. These two giants in the spiritual family tree of modern pastoral care believe that pastoral care includes caring for the community of faith and the wider society, in addition to caring for individuals.

Pamela Couture, a clergywoman and pastoral theology professor who has specialized in ministries relating to social issues and government policy, especially as they relate to women, has also been a key leader in advocating this broader understanding of pastoral care. As a result of her examination of social-justice issues, Couture urges pastors to notice how societal systems inhibit individuals'

personal growth. In particular, she emphasizes harmful effects that come from our culture's emphasis on self-sufficiency. "The problem with self-sufficiency as a norm for policy," she notes, "is that it conceals the interconnections between individuals, families, social institutions, and government, which are essential for human flourishing."[6] Because she believes these interconnections are essential and are in danger of being lost, Couture has helped the pastoral care movement to correct its earlier assumption that spiritual growth is merely an individual endeavor.

Sharing spiritual family trees confirms the fallacy of that assumption. When we share, we see that faith comes from being connected with family members and other people. We see that we aren't alone on the faith journey. We recall that others have also been on the journey and that, for good or ill, they have affected us.

For several reasons, then, sharing spiritual family trees can be valuable for

39

faith building in religious groups. Sharing spiritual family trees can help group members see not only their personal and spiritual roots but also how they might bond with others to deepen their faith journey and strengthen their faith community. This method of faith-community building will help to bind people together in a common goal of being better believers and better neighbors, whether they are Christians, Jews, or Muslims. Sharing spiritual family trees is an especially effective way of sharing in religious groups because it shows us how family background has influenced our way of participating in groups.

## Looking at the Whole System

Pastor Peter L. Steinke explains why using a family systems method is so useful. Like other advocates of such methods, he acknowledges that the church is not a family, but he also sees that it is an emotional system in which the same emotional processes experienced in the family are operating. Steinke therefore assures us that looking only at the individuals who make up a religious group is not enough. We must look at the whole system. "Basically, a system is a set of forces and events that interact, such as a weather system or the solar system," Steinke explains. "To think systematically is to look at the ongoing, vital interaction of the connected parts."[7]

"As long as people gather and interact," Steinke reminds us, "emotional processes occur. There are positive aspects of these processes—joy, comfort, support, cooperation, and friendship. But emotional systems are inherently anxious. The downside, therefore, is the intense anxiety that distracts the congregation from its purpose, sets people at odds with each other, and builds walls against outsiders." What church members therefore need to recognize, Steinke notes, isn't just the presence of anxiety in the church but also the harmful effect it can have on the church's ability to carry out its mission. "The key question is whether or not anxiety, so much a part of these processes, *infects* the relationship, bringing about discord and destruction."

What makes analyzing the church's emotional processes hard, Steinke explains, is that we may not even realize they exist. "Our primary dilemma," in Steinke's view, "is that emotional processes are difficult to observe. They are invisible, often beyond our awareness. . . . And, of course, their invisibility increases when we ourselves are involved in them."

After realizing that such processes exist, our job is to understand how they work and what part we're playing in them. But even understanding isn't enough. "Understanding," Steinke writes, "will not change these processes. But if understanding is translated into new ways of being and doing, emotional processes can be directed toward health and well-being as we live the divine vocation entrusted to us."

Steinke reminds us, too, that a group of people is more than the combined individual actions of its members. "The whole is a force in itself. It exerts a force greater than any of its composing pieces."[8] Here's how Rabbi Edwin H. Friedman puts it, in his foreword to Steinke's book. "The family model . . . is based on the idea that relationship systems are not built up out of the personalities of those who belong to them, but rather that the 'personalities' in any institution express themselves according to the forces within the system and their position within those forces."[9]

Gil Rendle, a clergyman and director of Consulting and Education for the Alban Institute, also emphasizes this characteristic of groups. He points out that groups have personalities just as individuals do, and that unlike most religious leaders, leaders in the secular world have been paying attention to this fact for a long time. He finds this ironic because in his opinion the idea of corporate personality originated in the church.[10]

41

Theologian Walter Wink finds the corporate personalities of early churches described in the New Testament book of Revelation, in its letters to seven churches in Asia Minor. Unlike the apostle Paul's letters, which were addressed to entire congregations, the letters in the book of Revelation are addressed to the angels of the churches. "It would appear," Wink notes, "that the angel is not something separate from the congregation, but must somehow represent it as a totality." In Wink's view, "the fact that the angel is actually addressed suggests that is it more than a mere personification of the church, but the actual spirituality of the congregation as a single entity." He explains further: "Angel and people are the inner and outer aspects of one and the same reality. . . . The one cannot exist without the other."[11] One is visible, and the other is invisible.

If Wink's observation is correct, what does it mean for our religious bodies? "If we want to change those systems," he writes, "we will have to address not only their outer forms, but their inner spirit as well." Wink includes a warning with his explanation: "The spirituality that we encounter in institutions is not always benign," he assures, "it is just as likely to be pathological."[12] Here's what he concludes about how to change the religious bodies and other groups we belong to: "If the demonic arises when an angel deviates from its calling, then social change does not depend on casting out the demon, but recalling its angel to its divine task."[13]

Gil Rendle observes that when people gather in a relationship with God, they form the corporate personality that religious language calls "community." It is a personality that changes over time as some people leave the group and others enter. The religious leader's job, in Rendle's view, is to help the group identify its personality. This is a process of corporate discernment, he says, in which members read themselves, their congregation, and the congregation's religious tradition in order to see how to blend those together.

This process is harder today than in previous times because the people coming into today's congregations are more diverse than those who came in earlier years. Like many other observers, Rendle finds that today's people aren't as likely as yesterday's to stick with their parents' religious traditions. Helping these diverse newcomers find their places in our religious groups now requires dialogue. According to Rendle, we must take individuals' insights and make them part of that dialogue.

Genograms, questionnaires for classifying personality types, and other such instruments, Rendle explains, can be powerful because they furnish a common language for talking about people's differences. Such instruments therefore help people move from a win-lose position with regard to differences, to a win-win position that lets individuals see how they can relate to the group. When people first use one of these instruments that help them recognize who they are, Rendle finds, they're likely to see their typical way of functioning as something the group must simply accept. Their reaction is usually "Why should anyone expect me to be different? This is the way I am." A good leader, says Rendle, helps them move toward the question "How can I make choices that will let me be part of this larger group?"[14]

In chapter 6 we'll look at how sharing spiritual family trees can encourage members of religious groups (and maybe social or professional groups, too) to ask this question. First, however, we need to look at how to draw a spiritual family tree and at why drawing instead of just speaking or writing is important.

## Looking Deeper

- What group(s) do you belong to, in which you'd like to know other members better or feel more a part of the group?

- If you're a pastor, what attitudes or beliefs of your members do you find difficult to cope with? Have you tried to discover members' reasons for holding those views?

- What role has sharing faith stories played in the history of your religious tradition?

- Do you share faith stories in your church or other religious group?

- If you're a lay person, do you feel that your pastor should give pastoral care only to church members or to the community outside the church as well?

- Have you ever used a personality questionnaire or other such instrument to identify your personality type or leadership style? If so, did you learn anything that affected your way of functioning or seeing yourself?

CHAPTER **4**

# Sharing Your Story

We've now explained the uses of genograms and the ways that sharing spiritual family trees can help religious groups build community, but you may be left with a question. Why draw a diagram when religious histories can be shared orally or in written form?

Genograms are helpful for the following reasons.

- Some people absorb information better visually.

- A diagram presents information quickly at a glance, which some people find easier than reading or listening to a lot of words.

- Some people learn more by doing than by hearing or seeing. The physical process of drawing a diagram can help these people become aware of and solidify the key features in their own stories.

- Genograms clearly show the relationship between members of different generations and between various family members. It's easy to get lost when someone merely talks about his aunt's husband or her first cousin once removed.

- Genograms may reveal certain characteristics that have been repeated through family members. For example, if you're male and your mother, grandmother, and great-grandmother were all active churchgoers and urged you to be, but all the males in your family were non-churchgoers who saw church activities only as something for "ladies," that pattern has probably had an important effect on you, one that you need to recognize.

So let's look at how to draw a spiritual family tree using genograms.

## Drawing Your Spiritual Family Tree

As we mentioned in chapter 1, specific shapes and lines denote gender and relation on a genogram. Figure 6 *(page 47)* shows these symbols. Before you draw your spiritual family tree, review this figure. Then start your genogram by using squares to represent males and circles to represent females. (If you're sharing your tree with a group, draw it on a board or a paper large enough for all to see.) Start near the bottom of the paper.

1. Draw a square and a circle side by side, with a short horizontal line connecting them, to represent your parents.

2. Below them, draw circles and squares beside each other to represent you and your brothers and sisters.

3. Connect yourself and your brothers and sisters to your parents with diagonal lines.

4. Add your grandparents above your parents.

5. Add spouses, aunts, uncles, cousins, and earlier generations if you wish, but include only the relatives with whom you've had a good bit of contact.

Connect people who lived together as partners, whether or not they were married. If you wish, indicate "living together" by putting "LT" on the connecting line, or simply use a dashed line. For couples who separated or divorced, put

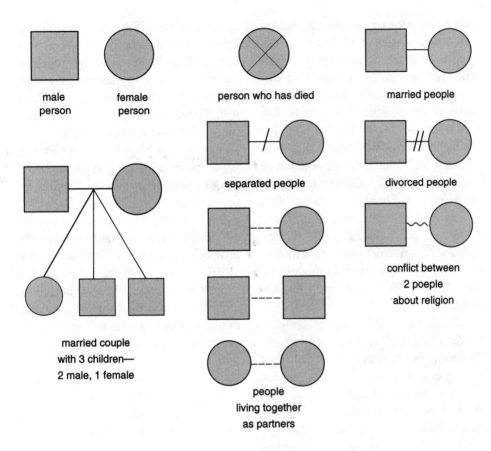

male person

female person

person who has died

married people

separated people

divorced people

conflict between 2 poeple about religion

married couple with 3 children— 2 male, 1 female

people living together as partners

**Figure 6. Explanation of symbols**

47

a slash across the connection line. If there was consistent conflict between two people about religious or spiritual matters, use a wavy line to connect them.

Label each square or circle with the name of the person it represents. Use actual names (Joe or Joe Williams) or use the names you call them (Dad, Mom, Gramps, and so on). For anyone whose name you don't know, leave the square or circle blank. For anyone who has died, put an X through the square or circle. Beside people's names, jot down their religious involvement or their influence on yours, for example, "Lutheran pastor," "active Methodist," or "read the Bible to me."

Around the family diagram, write the names of other people who strongly influenced your religious beliefs or practices: perhaps a teacher, pastor, special friend, or mentor. If certain experiences were especially important, jot them down. Perhaps church camp was especially enlightening, or maybe the Vietnam War or the civil rights movement strongly

influenced you. If these events, experiences, and non-family members were important in shaping your spiritual or religious life, you may want to draw a separate genogram for them. You could use a different symbol—a triangle, perhaps—for events and experiences. If something else played an important part in your spiritual history, as books did for Barbara, you might want to include a distinct symbol for that as well. Use whatever mixture of symbols best represents all these influences. Figure 7 *(page 49)* provides an example of Barbara's story.

Another way to record influential events and non-family members is to draw them on a time line of your life. Figure 8 shows a sample.

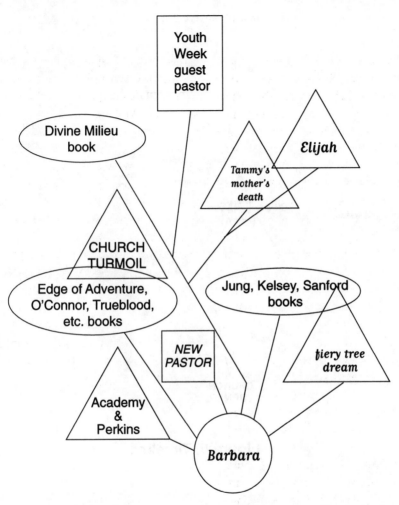

**Figure 7. Tree of events and non-family people**

49

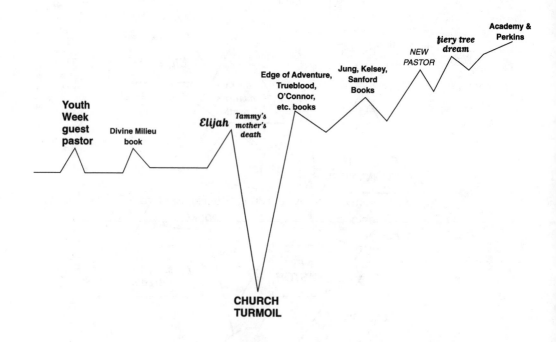

**Youth Week guest pastor**

**Divine Milieu book**

*Elijah*

*Tammy's mother's death*

**Edge of Adventure, Trueblood, O'Connor, etc. books**

**Jung, Kelsey, Sanford Books**

*NEW PASTOR*

*fiery tree dream*

**Academy & Perkins**

**CHURCH TURMOIL**

**Figure 8. Timeline**

You may find it helpful to use some kind of shorthand or symbol to differentiate between people whose influence seems positive and those whose influence seems negative. You might also consider using this kind of shorthand to indicate the person's attitude toward religion. For example, put plus signs (+) or checkmarks (✓) by the names of those who were helpful to you or were positive about religion, and minus signs (–) or x-marks (X) by those who hindered your spiritual growth or had a negative attitude about religion. By the name of someone who stands out as uniquely helpful—a shining star in your spiritual history—you might want to draw a star. You might also use a star to indicate an especially memorable or life-changing experience. Figure 9 *(page 52)* shows a sample of a spiritual family tree using such symbols.

If you draw your diagram in front of a group, talk about the key people in your tree and how they influenced your beliefs, spiritual growth, and religious habits. Invite listeners to ask questions so that they understand what you're saying. Their questions may also help you recall important events and people that you have forgotten.

# Questions to Ask Yourself

As you consider your spiritual history and draw your spiritual family tree, there are some important questions you may want to consider. Following are questions that Marsha Wiggins Frame suggests for therapists, which can also be useful in sharing spiritual family trees.

- When you were growing up, what role, if any, did religion or spirituality play in your life? What role does it play now?

- What specific religious or spiritual beliefs do you now consider most important? How are these beliefs a source of connection or conflict between you and other family members?

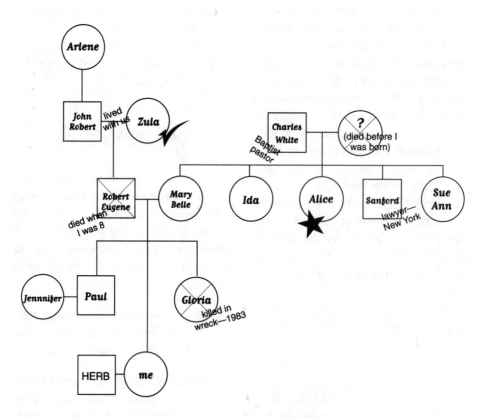

**Figure 9. Sample genogram**

52

- What religious or spiritual rituals did you participate in as a child or teenager? How important were they in your family of origin? Which ones do you still engage in? Which ones have you let go? What new rituals have you adopted as an adult? How do these connect to your religious/spiritual belief system?

- What did/does your religious or spiritual tradition say about gender? About ethnicity? About sexual orientation? How has this affected you and your extended family?

- What behavioral and relationship patterns from religion and spirituality emerge as you think about your genogram? How are you currently maintaining or avoiding those patterns?

- What new insights or solutions have you discovered in drawing your genogram?[1]

# Questions to Ask Family Members

Frame finds that drawing a religious genogram sometimes leads a client to contact family members in order to find out about events, meanings, and religious practices and beliefs. If drawing your spiritual family tree makes you aware of gaps or questions, you may want to get in touch with people who can help you fill the gaps you've found. Frame suggests asking those familiy members the following questions.

- How did you perceive the importance of religion or spirituality in our family?

- Did your experience of the religious or spiritual climate in our family differ from mine? If so, how?

- Which members of our extended family seem to have had the most power when it came to religion or spirituality? Which ones had the least? How do you think the use of this power affected our family and our relationships with each other?

- How hard do you think it has been or would be for family members to seek a spiritual or religious path different from the one we were raised with? Who would be supportive? Who would not be? Why?

- How do you think religion or spirituality has been a source of strength for our family? How do you think it has interfered in family relationships?[2]

If you share your spiritual family tree with a group, invite your listeners to offer their own observations about what you tell them. They are likely to notice things you hadn't, perhaps identifying key influences you considered insignificant or seeing patterns and meaning you missed. You'll probably be pleased and surprised to find out more about yourself, and knowing more will certainly benefit you in the long run. This process will also bring you closer to those you share it with.

If you've never been in a group that shared so openly, the kind of sharing described here may seem strange. It may seem too risky. We urge you to try it anyway. We all tend to avoid seeing difficult or uncomfortable aspects of our lives, but this avoidance keeps us from making those aspects available to God for healing and growth. Enlisting friends' help is a good way to discover things we'd otherwise overlook. Indeed, it was open sharing that helped make the Methodist movement so powerful in its early years, and throughout history numerous other religious groups have also found the power that comes through sharing personal stories. Only recently have religious groups become places where people mainly listen, or where they talk only about the same superficial topics that casual acquaintances talk about at social events.

# Ground Rules

Before starting to share spiritual family trees, it's important to establish clear ground rules about sharing. The leader needs to take responsibility for making these rules clear, not only when the process begins but also at the beginning of each session. It may also be necessary to remind participants of the rules during the sharing. Although not exhaustive, the following list of rules will get you started.

- Be open but selective. Don't reveal anything that the person you're talking about wouldn't want revealed. Be considerate of others' privacy and your own.

- Establish and preserve confidentiality. Group members need to agree that what they see and hear while sharing will stay within the group.

- Don't try to solve personal problems that become apparent during the sharing. Remember, the purpose of sharing spiritual family trees in a religious or social group is to build intimacy and community, not therapy.

This last rule deserves some discussion. In earlier chapters we've said a lot about how genograms are used in therapy, but sharing spiritual family trees in religious groups is different. Clients come to therapy to address problems and relieve suffering, both for the client and for those with whom he or she has contact. The goal of sharing spiritual family trees is mainly to build community in which members know and care about each other and work together to carry out a God-given purpose. This kind of sharing helps members become more effective in contributing to the group's shared goals. When this happens, group participation and ownership increase. Members begin to feel part of the group and to have a sense of responsibility for what happens in it.

# Getting Prepared

If you're going to lead a sharing session, be sure to get all the necessary materials ready beforehand. If participants will draw in front of the group, you will need chalk or dry markers and an eraser for the board, or felt-tip pens, an easel, and a large paper tablet. Be sure the board or tablet is high enough and writing utensils dark enough for all participants to see easily. Arrange seating so that everyone can see.

You may want to provide paper and pens for participants. Listeners and presenters may want to write down thoughts triggered by the sharing. And depending on the presentation schedule, participants may need paper on which to draw their trees during a quiet time before sharing begins.

In addition to getting all the necessary materials ready ahead of time, mental and spiritual preparation is also important, for the leader as well as the other participants. Consider opening each sharing session with prayer and perhaps a brief time of silence or guided meditation. Ask God to guide the process, to help participants recall what they want to share, and to help them be receptive to what others share.

As a leader, your preparation should also include reminding yourself to avoid exerting inappropriate power over the group during the sharing. Part of a leader's responsibility is to make sure that no participant feels quashed or unappreciated because of anything he or she reveals. You must defend any participant who is in the minority in the group for any reason, by helping the majority to consider that person's views and experiences rather than overpower him or her with majority viewpoints. Beyond that, the leader's role is the same as in any group: make sure that participants play fair, be sure everyone who wants to be heard gets a chance, and help group members respect each other. Last but not least, remember that the leader's role is to lead, not to be an expert who delivers advice or information.

After reading this far, you may simply want to draw your spiritual family tree and think about it by yourself rather than share it with anyone. Doing it alone would be more helpful to you than not doing it at all, certainly, but sharing it with someone close to you would be even more helpful, and sharing it with a group could be the most helpful of all. We hope you'll try it. We think you'll find some welcome kindred spirits. We think you'll feel closer to God, too.

In the next chapter we'll explore some of the benefits of group sharing and we'll look at some specifics of leading a group.

# Looking Deeper

- How do you best absorb information or learn a skill? By hearing, seeing, or doing?

- In your family, what attitudes toward religion were typical of the men? Of the women?

- Which of the suggested "Questions to Ask Yourself" have you considered before? Which ones do you find most helpful?

- Which of the "Questions to Ask Family Members" have you asked your family members? Does asking them seem threatening or helpful?

- In the religious groups you belong to, do people mainly listen or do they actively participate? Are members' conversations with each other superficial or do they talk about real concerns and interests? Would you welcome deeper conversation or does that seem too risky?

CHAPTER 5

# Leading Your Group

Now that we've looked at the specifics of sharing spiritual family trees and preparing for a sharing session, it's time to consider how to design and lead the process in a way that will help your group become an effective part of the church or other religious organization.

We start with Larry's experience as a leader. For the last 20 years he has led groups in various settings in Clinical Pastoral Education (CPE). Sharing spiritual family trees in these groups helps group members focus on their own experiences as well as those of their learning companions, and thus work together more effectively.

Each of these groups was composed of five or six people who had committed themselves to each other and to the learning of pastoral-care skills. Their CPE program lasted 12 weeks, one year, or in some cases, two to three years. Sharing spiritual family trees almost always helped the groups learn more about themselves and the other group members. Quite often that sharing has sparked curiosity and close connections between group members. The sharing process quickly establishes the openness that promotes personal relationships.

## Group Building: A Case Study

The retreat described here is a composite of many groups that Larry has facilitated. Participants' names and details of their spiritual family trees have been altered here to preserve confidentiality. However, this description accurately shows the potential of spiritual family trees in group building. Here's how Larry describes the experience.

This group was composed of six persons, including me as facilitator. We were to be together for at least the next year, working together as chaplains. We would be a team caring for the needs of patients, families, and staff in a large teaching hospital.

After meeting each other and becoming familiar with the hospital policies and procedures we would follow during the coming year, we went on a day-long retreat to begin the process of getting to know each other better.

The retreat started with a 20-minute chapel service that I led. Members shared some prayers for the life of the group. Some members expressed thoughts and feelings about facing the unknown and beginning a new experience. After the chapel service and some donuts and coffee, we began the process of sharing ourselves and our experiences through the use of spiritual family trees.

First I shared my own tree, as I described it in chapter 1 of this book. Before I started, however, I assured the other group members that even though I'd previously shared my tree several times, I was sure I would learn more about myself this time. Each time I share it I tend to see something new.

The process of drawing my spiritual family tree on a board and telling the group about it took about 30 minutes. Then I allowed another 15 minutes for questions and comments, because I wanted to hear people's responses and learn something new.

After we'd finished talking about my spiritual family tree, we took a break so that group members could draw their own. When we came back together, each person redrew his or her tree on the board and talked about what it meant.

## Janet

Janet volunteered to share hers first *(see figure 10 on page 62)*. She was in her mid 40s, Euro-American, married, and a United Methodist clergywoman. At the time of the retreat she and her husband had three late-teenage children. Janet said she was interested in chaplaincy as a career.

Janet told us she was the oldest of three children, all female. Her father was a businessman and her mother worked in real estate. Her family had belonged to the Methodist Church for generations. She believed that one of her great-grand-fathers was an itinerant Methodist minister.

Janet talked about her mother's and father's involvement in their local United Methodist church, including the church events and activities they participated in—the same kinds of events in which she also participated. Then she paused for a moment. Seeing how many times she'd written "Sunday School teacher" by the names of family members, she laughed and said, "My goodness! Until I saw what I've put on this diagram, I'd never realized how many people in my family taught Sunday School." Then her face became somber. "I just realized," she said quietly, "that my parents and I over-commit ourselves in church activities. I believe this is because we want to live out our faith, but I'm aware of how tired I get and how much I long for rest." As she talked, I noticed several group members nodding their heads in recognition and agreement.

Janet went on to talk about her husband, who was a successful physician, and her three children. She was quite proud of her children, she assured us, "They are good kids." She then talked about how hard it was for her to go to school, raise children, and pursue ordination all at the same time. She explained that even though the United Methodist Church was more open to women's ordination than some faith traditions, her journey had still been difficult.

After group members questioned Janet for a few minutes, Lee volunteered to share.

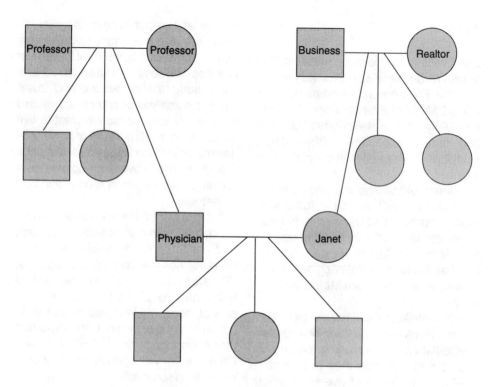

Janet is from the midwest, United Methodist
minister, well to do, and on her second
career, after raising children.

**Figure 10. Janet's genogram**

## Lee

Lee, in his mid 40s and from Southeast Asia, had never been married *(see figure 11 see page 64)*. He came to the United States to pursue education and to become a Presbyterian minister. He told of growing up in a region plagued by constant conflict. Most of the people in his culture were Buddhist, so as a Christian he was in the minority. He told of beatings that some of his friends had received for being Christian.

There had been a war in Lee's country 30 years ago. His grandfather, his father, and two of his three uncles had been killed in the war. He was too young at the time to witness any of the killing, but he remembered the profound sadness he felt when he was told that his father had been killed.

After Lee's father died, a group of his neighbors, Presbyterians, helped his mother and his three sisters with clothes and food until his mother could find a better job. "At first I was embarrassed to be seen with Christians," he said, "but over time their kindness won me and my family over." He went on to go to Christian schools and then connected with missionaries who helped him come to the United States.

Everyone in the group was somber and even sad when Lee finished sharing his experiences. After asking him a few questions, we broke for lunch and then some quiet time until we met again in the afternoon.

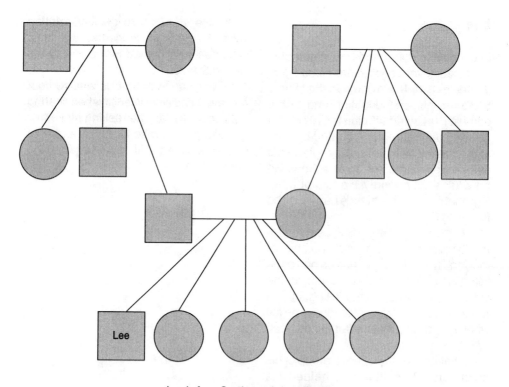

Lee is from Southeast Asia, a Buddhist
war-torn society, a Christian, and a Presbyterian minister.

## Figure 11. Lee's genogram

## Mary

Mary offered to go first after the break (*see figure 12 page 66*). She was in her mid 30s, African American, and from the southeastern United States. Recently ordained by her local Pentecostal church, she said that the Holy Spirit had led her into chaplaincy.

Mary started by saying, "Lee, I don't know what it's like to grow up in a war-torn country, but I do know what it's like to grow up as a minority." Then she went on to talk about experiences she had with prejudice. The group was appalled. She noted that her worst experience with prejudice had been in a restaurant in the north. This surprised us. For many of us, Mary's experiences were so foreign that they were hard to imagine.

Mary talked about how all of the members of her family belonged to the same church. This apparently caused some conflict in the family, but mostly the church was a nurturing place, a place to "recharge the batteries." In worship, Mary told us, she could always count on God "lifting her up," no matter how bad her week had been.

We asked her a few questions about the civil rights movement and her church's involvement. She told us about her church's history in the movement. Although most of the work had been in the '50s and '60s, before she was born, struggles for equality and justice were still going on.

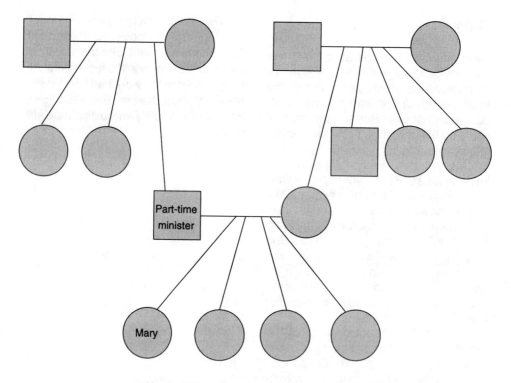

Mary is African American, Pentecostal, from the
southeast, and with a family all in the same congregation.

**Figure 12. Mary's genogram**

## Elizabeth

Elizabeth was next *(see figure 13 on page 68).* She was a Euro-American in her early 30s and grew up in the Northeast. Her family was Episcopalian and had been for generations. Both of her grandfathers were bankers and both of her grandmothers were teachers. Her father was a businessman and her mother was a teacher. She remembers her family as being very formal. "Until I saw my family tree drawn in this way, and told all of you about it," she said, "I hadn't really realized how lukewarm most of my family seemed about the church."

When Elizabeth was 13 she went to a boarding school. There she met a chaplain who became her mentor. In contrast to her family, he wasn't at all lukewarm about the church. He would ask Elizabeth difficult questions, and she always enjoyed the depth of their discussions. "The most alive times of my life," she said, "were times when we (the chaplain and I) talked about the meaning of life." I also remember the power of the Eucharist," she told us. "The wafer, when broken, thundered with electricity and power." She later became involved in Greenpeace and interested in the Episcopal priesthood.

We asked Elizabeth about boarding school, as none of the rest of us had experienced it. And we wanted to know more about the power of the sacrament for her, as well as about her experience with Greenpeace.

67

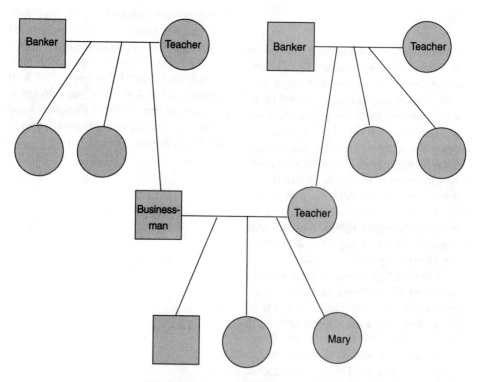

Elizabeth is from the northeast, Episcopalian
and attended boarding school.

## Figure 13. Elizabeth's genogram

## Jim

Finally it was Jim's turn *(see figure 14 on page 70)*. Jim was a 25-year-old, Euro-American, Southern Baptist minister. His father was a Baptist minister and his father's father was a Baptist minister. Both of them were mentors for Jim. He identified with what Janet had told us about her parents' "workaholism" (his word) because he felt his father was like that, spending more time at the church than at home. Jim wondered if he, too, was headed in that direction.

Jim courageously confessed that he didn't believe women should be ordained. He therefore wondered about being in a group with three ordained women. The tension in the room went up a bit, but the other group members appreciated Jim's courage and honesty, and this helped to set a valuable tone for openness.

The Baptist church had been central in his life. Jim realized that this was his first time in a group of non-Baptists. He said that he hoped we would accept him. He also apologized to Mary for the Southern Baptist Church's persecution of African Americans in the South. He seemed genuinely pained by what his church had done in the last two centuries. Mary graciously but cautiously accepted Jim's apology.

After Jim shared his tree, someone mentioned that all the family members he had described as strong leaders were men, indicated by squares on the genogram. Jim hadn't thought about this before.

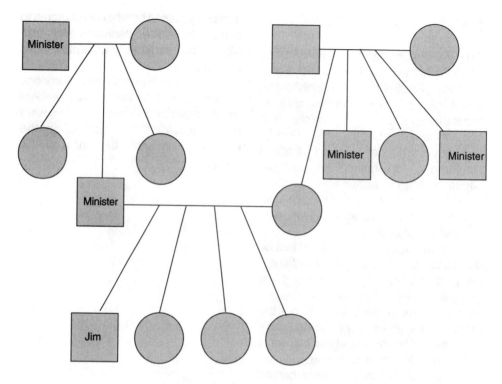

Jim is from southern U.S., is Southern Baptist, and
does not believe in ordination of women.

**Figure 14. Jim's genogram**

## Beginning Deeper Relationships

In summarizing our retreat, we noted how diverse our group was, and how interesting and sometimes profound our spiritual family trees were. Jim said that he had always wondered about non-Baptists but had found our group's spiritual journeys genuinely moving. We all agreed that Lee had had an amazingly difficult journey, and we wondered if he would be more helpful for people in crisis because of having experienced such great difficulties himself.

Mary commented on how accepted she felt in our group. As an African American, she said, "I always look and see if I will be part of the group or not." She said she was looking forward to learning more about each of us. Everyone agreed that sharing spiritual family trees was an excellent way to start building deeper relationships and that the retreat was a good way to begin the year we were to spend together.

As the year progressed, the themes that emerged during the retreat continued to emerge as our group relationship developed. We focused quite a bit on the ordination of women, and by the end of the year Jim had become more open to the issue. He said, "I saw the powerful ministry of the women in the group."

All of us Westerners had difficulty understanding Lee's Eastern patterns of relationship. He helped us learn a great deal about Asian culture. Mary helped us understand her perspective as well. The racial issue emerged again and again as all of us witnessed the inequality of race in our culture.

Other issues kept reemerging, too. Janet repeatedly confronted us with overworking and spreading ourselves too thin. With her help we were able to look at our own work-family priorities. Through Elizabeth's experience we were able to confront the divide between the rich and the poor.

Our relationships with each other deepened over the year, but the process was not easy. We had many ups and downs. At the end of the year when we evaluated our time together, we all pointed back to the sharing of our spiritual family trees as having gotten us off to a strong start—a start that continually helped us move forward and become closer as a group.

# Your Group

After reading Larry's description of the retreat and how he used spiritual family trees as its centerpiece, what ideas do you have about how you might do something similar in a religious group you belong to? What if your group is larger than his? What if your group isn't willing or able to give a whole day to the process? What if it can give more time, including some follow-up at later meetings?

Nancy, a lay church member, incorporated the tree-sharing process into a weekend retreat attended by 25 people. At the end of an afternoon session she distributed brief instructions for drawing and sharing spiritual family trees, telling the group a little about the process and its benefits as she distributed the handouts. Next she gave each member a large, blank sheet of paper to use for their trees. She suggested that each participant go to his or her room or some other private place during the evening, to think and draw, and that at the next morning's session all who were willing could share what they had drawn. The next morning everyone shared with the whole group.

This is a good method, especially for a retreat. As the leader, give participants a brief description and instructions in advance, being sure to emphasize that participants should focus on religious and spiritual aspects of their family histories. You might also want to hand out written descriptions and instructions, and a sheet of paper (8 1/2 x 11 inches or larger) to draw on before the retreat. Then, when the time comes to share during the retreat, participants can quickly copy their trees onto a board or flip chart for all to see.

If participants feel uncomfortable sharing in front of a lot of people, or if the time available for sharing is short, a larger group can be divided into smaller groups for the sharing. One laywoman divided the 20 or so people in her Sunday School class into groups of four or five when sharing time came. Larry has used similar methods for groups he has led.

In any group setting, the leader should share his or her own tree before other members share. This helps participants feel more comfortable with the process and shows them clearly what they will be expected to do. It also gives them the chance to ask questions about the process. At a retreat or other gathering where all participants will share during one session, the leader should share first and then have the group adjourn for a break, during which they can draw their own spiritual family trees. Group sharing can start after the break.

As leader, you might include some quiet, solitary time for reflection after the sharing. During this time participants can journal or doodle, or create a poem or sketch inspired by their own or others' spiritual family trees—whatever they feel called to do. This time is for personal reflection. After going through the process of creating and sharing their spiritual family trees, participants are likely to need it.

You might also suggest that each group member jot down a one- or two-sentence statement about what they consider the most important insight they've gained from the process. This could be a good way to end the session, especially if your meeting time is short. Then if time permits, you might invite each person who was willing to read his or her statement to the group as a conclusion to your time together.

## Going Further

What about follow-up? It's important to consider. How can you build on what you and your group accomplished by drawing and sharing spiritual family trees?

Even if participants share only partially with the group, they're likely to find the process of drawing and reflecting on a spiritual family tree valuable. For one thing, the process prepares you for sharing parts of your story with individuals or groups that you later have occasion to speak to. Drawing and reflecting on a spiritual family tree can help you share your faith more effectively, whether in a personal conversation or a public presentation. Drawing squares, circles, lines, and symbols may not seem essential, but it will help you tell your story in a concise, complete, and meaningful way for your listeners. If you're a pastor, the process could help to prepare you for including parts of your history in sermons, other presentations, and one-on-one conversations.

If your group is a leadership team that will work together for an extended period of time, it is helpful to spend some time in an initial session reflecting on what you have learned through sharing spiritual family trees. This is especially true if your group comprises top leaders of a congregation, church denomination, or other religious organization. People in these groups probably have the greatest opportunity and power to influence the future direction of an entire organization. Taking this reflection a step further, group members might also benefit from an initial brainstorming session.

Ideas developed in this session will feed later sessions, during which group members will look at the organization's purpose and resources, and form plans for leadership roles and responsibilities.

If all participants are knowledgeable about the religious organization and are experienced in its leadership roles, after everyone has shared it may be helpful to identify issues or themes revealed during sharing that are of special concern in the current life of the organization. These issues and themes can be listed on a board and then future gatherings can focus on themes that turn out to be of the greatest concern for all. These themes are often controversial, ranging from the small, such as whether to use crackers or a common loaf for communion, to the larger ones, such as worship style and how to deal with major social-justice issues. Finally, discovering pieces of participants' spiritual journeys may reveal new ministries or worship practices that need to be added to your group's corporate life.

## Your Congregation's Spiritual History

Like individuals, congregations also have spiritual histories. Drawing your congregation's spiritual family tree might prove helpful. You might identify people who have been the congregation's spiritual ancestors: the founding pastor, perhaps, or lifelong members who have taken responsibility for the congregation's building or finances. Events can be spiritual ancestors, too: moving to a new building, a sudden population growth in the community, a tornado that did major damage, the closing of a business on which many members depended for their income, the unexpected death of a dynamic pastor who everyone assumed would be the pastor forever, and so on.

Consider how these people and events have affected the congregation's beliefs and attitudes. Like personal spiritual ancestors, congregational ancestors can inspire or discourage us. They can limit our horizons or expand them. They can show us paths that will lead us closer to God, or keep us from discovering those paths. They can help us find the ministries to which God calls us, either as a congregation or as individual members of it, or they can contribute to our lack of awareness about our gifts and callings. How could you as a religious leader help your group look at these aspects of its spiritual ancestry? Could you do it in a way that would move the group toward God's intended future?

An invaluable result of sharing spiritual family trees is the resolution of conflicts within the group. Another is the discovery of better ways to make decisions as a group. We'll look at these kinds of results in the next chapter.

## Looking Deeper

- Have you ever heard someone tell about experiencing the effects of racial or religious prejudice? If so, how were you affected by the similarity to or difference from your own experience?

- As you read members' stories from Larry's CPE group, what struck you? How do their stories compare to yours?

- Elizabeth said that her "most alive times" in life were conversations with her mentor about the meaning of life. When in your life have you felt most alive? What made you feel so alive?

- In your group, how could you help others feel more accepted?

# CHAPTER 6

# Turning Conflict into Cooperation

In any personal relationship, conflict is inevitable. It is also inevitable in groups. Any attempt to build intimate relationships will include misunderstandings, tension, and miscommunication. Sharing spiritual family trees, however, can help to ease tensions.

When we share spiritual family trees, participants become aware of how family members and other spiritual ancestors have influenced their expectations about how religious groups should function. This is particularly valuable when spiritual family trees are shared as part of conflict resolution processes and in church councils, visioning groups, and other decision-making groups within religious organizations. Group participants come to see how and why other participants have developed different expectations, and that no set of expectations is necessarily wrong or right. Sharing spiritual family trees can help participants gain valuable perspective in discussions of communion practices, for example, and of other worship practices about which members have strong but different views and preferences.

The broader perspective that comes from sharing spiritual family trees is especially valuable in today's church. In contrast to the churches of earlier years, congregants now come from a variety of religious backgrounds and tend to move freely from one denomination to another. This change alone has increased the influence of two major, conflict-building obstacles. In fact, in his 20 years as a chaplain and pastoral psychotherapist, Larry has found these two obstacles the greatest hindrances to building relationships.

1. *Expectations.* All of us have expectations about what a relationship ought to be. Some we have examined but many we have not. These expectations almost always come from our family of origin. To our religious groups, then, we bring not only expectations from our family background about how people should relate to each other individually and in groups, but also expectations about what religious groups should believe and do.

2. *Listening.* When we talk with someone with whom we want a relationship, we often feel that the other person is not listening. When we feel that someone is not listening to us, we feel devalued. We also feel cut off from a possible relationship with this person. This inhibits community building, which is one of the vital functions of spiritual life.

Sharing spiritual family trees can help to overcome these obstacles. Sharing spiritual family trees helps to reveal and explore group members' expectations, which prevents them from being such an obstacle. Also, because group members really listen to each person sharing his or her spiritual family tree, those sharing feel heard, valuable, and part of the group.

# A Clash of Expectations

Sharing spiritual family trees significantly reduced the influence of these two hindrances in an adult Sunday School class for which Larry once led a series of lessons on the theology of John Wesley. At the last session in the series, class members were discussing Wesleyan beliefs about the meaning of the eucharist—the sacrament of communion—and the ways in which Methodists practice it.

Suddenly a passionate debate erupted among class members, about how communion was observed in their congregation. The usual practice was for successive groups of worshipers to come to the altar rail, spend a very brief time there, and then be dismissed with a blessing by the officiating pastor. Some class members thought this method was fine, but others felt strongly that it did not allow enough time to pray at the altar. Some found the communion process unsanitary because participants shared a common loaf from which the pastor broke off bite-size pieces for each person. These class members thought the congregation should use the tiny, hard, commercially made communion wafers instead. Others insisted that those wafers do not qualify as bread, which led others to complain that the typical Methodist grape juice doesn't qualify as wine.

After this debate had raged on for a while, Larry realized that many of the class members might not have been Methodists for very long. "What is your faith tradition background?" he asked each person in the group. As you might suspect, some were originally Lutheran, some Southern Baptist, some Catholic, some Church of Christ, some Disciples of Christ, some Episcopal, and some from other denominations. Of the 25 people in the room, only five had grown up in the Methodist church. The conflict about communion practices, Larry realized, was actually about strong feelings that grew out of childhood experiences in different Christian traditions. Understandably, many class members still cherished these traditions.

Once the class recognized and acknowledged their diverse heritage, the dialogue became less impassioned. It quickly turned to each person sharing his or her childhood experiences of the eucharist. Even the names for this sacrament reflected differences in group members' spiritual histories and expectations. Some called the sacrament "communion," some called it "Holy Communion," some called it the "Lord's Supper," and some called it the "eucharist."

Even the lifelong Methodists, it

turned out, hadn't all experienced communion in the same way. Some had come from Methodist congregations that used loaves of bread, while others had used wafers. Some had come from congregations in which everyone knelt at the altar to be served, while others were used to walking by a server and dipping their bread into a cup held by the server. Some had come from congregations in which members filed out of their pews in order and waited in line to go to the altar. Some had come from the present church's tradition, in which groups of communicants went to the altar and were formally dismissed by the pastor with a blessing. Still others were used to having everyone go and come at will. No wonder there had been such impassioned disagreement among class members! Each one was using a different standard to measure what was right and what was wrong about a feature they all considered a vital part of being Christian.

## Inspiring Cooperation

Let's look at another conflict. Through the sharing of spiritual family trees, this conflict turned into cooperation, which led to exciting plans for the group's future.

Linda, a laywoman active in her church, really didn't want the job as president of her church's regional organization for women. She'd done lots of church jobs and was ready for a rest. Besides, stress, bitterness, and fighting were rampant in the organization, and she didn't want the responsibility of trying to get a group like that to do anything. To make matters worse, the outgoing president was domineering and autocratic, so members would surely resent whoever had the job next. Because she was a devoted, longtime member of the organization, Linda didn't want to see it collapse, so she agreed to become president.

The first event at which she would preside didn't look the least bit promising. It was an officers' retreat that the outgoing president had scheduled without telling Linda or consulting any of the other officers who would be expected to attend. Linda dreaded it for weeks before it happened.

She had recently read a book about the importance of spirituality for leadership, as well as some of Barbara's writing about sharing spiritual family trees, and she thought she could use some of this information to handle the meeting. It needed to start with some kind of spiritual focus, Linda thought. "I wanted a way to put away the garbage and make a fresh start." She decided to try sharing spiritual family trees. To her delight it worked.

Linda opened the meeting by briefly reviewing the book she had liked so much and then giving each member a copy of it. Then in late afternoon she gave everyone a large sheet of paper and a copy of Barbara's newsletter about sharing spiritual family trees. Linda briefly described the process and then shared her own tree. She asked attenders to go to private places that evening and draw their spiritual family trees. She told them they would share their trees at the next morning's session and that she would like everyone to take part although no one would be required to.

The sharing started right after breakfast. Each woman arrived prepared, and each one gladly shared her tree. To Linda's surprise and delight, they found the process so exciting that she had a hard time getting them to stop for lunch. The whole morning was filled with tears, laughter, and sharing, which Linda feels sure could never have happened otherwise. Many of the women found that others had experiences similar to their own. "I thought I was the only one who felt that way!" they kept saying as the morning progressed.

"It was so exciting to see them bond," Linda reports. And the lunchtime that followed, she says, was like nothing she had ever seen. They kept talking about what they had said and heard during the morning, and urging one another to say more, to explore the feelings and experiences they now realized they had in common. Most of the women hadn't really known each other before the meeting, Linda found, even though many of them had been regularly attending these meetings for years. At previous meetings she had noticed that members didn't talk much to each other. Even during mealtimes they didn't talk about anything except the business discussed that day. Now all that had changed, in a big way.

The group's business session came in the afternoon, and Linda says it also was like never before. Members were excitedly volunteering for jobs and suggesting new methods and projects. All were eager to get started doing the jobs they had been enlisted to do for the coming year. Several left saying, "I can't wait till our next meeting!" After she got home, Linda kept getting phone calls and e-mails from the members, suggesting new things to do and volunteering to do them.

Linda can still hardly believe what a change has come over the group, but she loves it. She's delighted to be president of such an eager and productive group. Now, she says, "you feel like they are all your family." And she knows that other members share these feelings.

One member's husband died unexpectedly soon after that meeting, and she was amazed and thrilled to get many letters and calls from widows in the group. Having told of their own experience of becoming widowed, and having heard others describe the pain it had also brought to them, these women saw the need to support one another in their grief. Because they understood the pain and isolation of becoming a widow, they wanted to help their newly discovered friend.

## Helping the Whole Congregation

Linda is now eager to use the spiritual family tree process again. She has been helping a new church congregation get established, and she wants to start a women's group in it. She feels that sharing spiritual family trees will be an ideal way to bring its members into real community when the group begins.

Linda is also thinking about ways in which the tree-sharing process could help a whole congregation. Remembering how members are often asked to mention "joys and concerns" just before congregational prayer in worship services, she sees how much more meaningful this practice could be if members had previously shared spiritual family trees. If someone reported the death of an especially cherished aunt or grandfather, for example, congregation members who had heard about that beloved and influential person as part of a spiritual family tree would recognize the significance of that person's death.

Every time Linda talks about sharing spiritual family trees now, she comes up with more situations in which it would help. "Thank you for this team-building tool!" she says over and over. "It's a wonder!"

## Reducing Conflict: Basic Principles

These glowing reports of conflict resolution may sound as if we're claiming magic power for the process of sharing spiritual family trees. Rest assured, we're not. The above examples merely illustrate how this sharing process makes especially effective use of several principles that religious groups often use to reduce conflict.

- The process increases group members' trust in the group leader. In sharing spiritual family trees, the leader shares his or her story first. This openness and willingness to risk being vulnerable, and seeing that doing so is safe, fosters trust.

83

- Through the process of sharing, group members come to see the leader as one of them. They realize that, like them, the leader has both struggles and triumphs. They also see that, like them, the leader has a personal story that ties into the larger, sacred story of the group's faith tradition.

- The sharing process helps the leader know the group members better. He or she becomes aware of their attitudes, values, assumptions, and feelings, along with painful life events and difficult experiences. This awareness can help the leader know better how to minister to them, or at least how to converse with them. The process thus helps to foster real and close relationships between the leader and individual group members. Discovering how resistances and biases originated also enables the leader to become more sympathetic.

- In the sharing process members' continuing spiritual struggles are revealed.

This awareness can encourage a covenant in which group members pledge to support each other and hold each other accountable as they work through their spiritual challenges together.

- Sharing spiritual family trees brings formerly unconscious feelings of anxiousness to consciousness for the individual as well as the group. Understanding and acknowledging anxiety can help the group become less anxious as a body. It also lets members know each other's particular anxiety-producing experiences and recognize them when they show up in church activities. In the heated communion debate described above, for example, class anxiety started to decrease only when class members began to see the importance of each member's sacred experience of communion.

- Sharing spiritual family trees is, in effect, a process of corporate discernment. In it, group members examine themselves, their congregation, and the congregation's religious tradition in order to see how to blend as a group. The process leads members to say, "I am a real member of this group. I am a real member of this faith tradition. I am a real member of this congregation." And the process lets them become aware of why they're members. It also motivates them to move the group forward so that they and other members can keep feeling a part of it. Finally, the process motivates group members to ask themselves, "How can I make choices that will let me be part of the group, both now and in the future?"

We hope that seeing how sharing spiritual family trees can reduce conflict and help in decision making will encourage you to use this process in some of your religious groups. Given the current emphasis on team building for staffs, officers, and work groups in all kinds of organizations, a spiritually based team-building tool is both appropriate and useful. Are you in a religious group where a difference in viewpoints is keeping the members from working together or even feeling kindly toward each other? Sharing spiritual family trees could help.

# Follow-up

For groups involved in decision making, it may be helpful to consider incorporating follow-up into the process of sharing spiritual family trees. Additional steps may help the group work together more effectively and with less conflict. One such step is leading group members through the process of discovering their personality types and spiritual gifts. *Please Understand Me*, by David Keirsey and Marilyn Bates,[1] explains the important influence of personality type differences in all groups. It includes a simple questionnaire for identifying your own personality type, and it describes how innate personality types cause people to receive and respond to information differently. These authors' later book *Please Understand Me II*[2] goes into the subject more fully.

*Discover Your Spiritual Type*, by Corinne Ware,[3] explains how personality type differences show up in religious groups in particular, including why people create conflict, seem to hinder decision making, or simply become apathetic and drop out. Ware also offers an excellent, easy-to-use group tool called The Spirituality Wheel. She even includes slightly different versions of it for Protestant, Catholic, and Jewish groups. Ware gives suggestions for individual meditation as well as concrete workshop schedules and programming for leading a congregation or decision-making group through the process of looking at spiritual types and their influence. Another helpful book on personality differences in religious groups is *Personality Type in Congregations*, by Lynne M. Baab.[4]

Becoming aware of personality differences and their roles in decision making and conflict can go a long way toward making a group an effective, harmonious, productive unit. When done in conjunction with sharing spiritual family trees, so that group members become aware of each other's different experiences and expectations at the same time, the results can be dramatic. Leading a group in recognizing and appreciating members' spiritual gifts can also be a helpful follow-up to sharing spiritual family trees, and several guides are widely available.

## Sharing in Other Situations

What kind of decision-making situations in your congregation or other religious group might be helped by sharing spiritual family trees? Such a process can be especially valuable in policy making, over which conflict is likely to arise. What about selecting a new pastor or other staff members for your congregation?

Recognizing the differing spiritual histories that lead to committee members' widely differing expectations and preferences about what a pastor should be could make a big difference in how the committee functions. Looking at the congregation's spiritual history could also be helpful for such a committee. It could help in a building or properties committee, too, in which members may have widely differing expectations about how a church building should look.

Sharing spiritual family trees can be especially helpful when controversial social issues threaten to cause major conflict. In a group that includes members of different sexual orientations, for example, sharing could be an important step toward reducing tensions, particularly in a group where church policies about the relation of sexual orientation to ordination and ministry will be discussed. Sharing in racially diverse groups could be similarly valuable in seeing why racial tension exists and how to lessen it.

Some Christians see churches' use of all-masculine language for referring to God and to human beings as harmful and totally inappropriate. Others see the issue as unimportant. Still others believe that any change would be heresy. Sharing spiritual family trees in a group of men and women, who are likely to have an assortment of views on this explosive issue, could be an important step toward agreeing on a church policy with regard to the issue.

An important part of being a leader is helping group members deal with decision making, controversy, and conflict in ways that allow members to work together for the good of the whole group and its purpose. Sharing spiritual family trees, especially used in conjunction with other group processes that promote awareness and mutual understanding, could go a long way toward helping you to be the leader that your group needs and that God wants you to be.

Now, before we review what some people have learned from creating and sharing spiritual family trees, in the next chapter we look briefly at how drawing and sharing a spiritual family tree might foster personal spiritual growth.

# Looking Deeper

- Have you ever felt differently about a person after discovering what contributed to his or her expectations or beliefs? Have you been more tolerant or agreed with those views?

- Do you belong to a religious organization in which sharing spiritual family trees might be welcome?

- What issues might your religious group deal with more effectively if members knew more about each other's spiritual history?

CHAPTER 7

# Growing in Faith

God has an infinite number of children but no grandchildren, it seems. We don't get faith or become Christian merely by having Christian parents or growing up in a Christian household. Our family may start us in useful religious habits and encourage us to continue them, but to be Christians we must make our own decisions and commitments. We must connect directly with God.

The Holy Spirit plays a crucial role in our faith journey. Many people make religious commitments despite being in a family with no religious involvement. Some become strongly committed even though family members try to discourage them. Spiritual family trees therefore don't tell anywhere near the whole

story of our faith and where it comes from. Still, looking at our spiritual family trees can play an important part in showing us where both the Holy Spirit and human influences (which may come about because of the Holy Spirit) are at work in our lives.

## Learning from Your Spiritual History

Through sharing spiritual family trees, members of our Sunday School class grew closer and became more aware of how our faith had grown. We learned some things about how faith matures. We became more aware of what had led us to our present attitudes about

Christianity and the institutional church. We saw some reasons for our having arrived at our present religious beliefs and our ways of acting on them.

When we are young our parents and other close family members do a lot to shape our religious habits, beliefs, and attitudes. That influence probably never leaves us completely, but others beyond our families may help us revise our childhood views and habits. These people are our spiritual ancestors, even though they're not members of our biological family. They have become part of our spiritual ancestry.

For some members of our class the most influential spiritual ancestor was a pastor. For others it was a Sunday School teacher, and for others a youth director. For some it was a college professor. For some it was an older friend they admired. Many of us have several important spiritual ancestors who aren't related to our biological family.

When the religious views we inherited from our home, our church, or our family's religious tradition were satisfying, these outsiders may have simply affirmed those views. If our inherited views were not convincing, however, outside people and events may have given us a different and more satisfying view. They offered a convincing alternative that we hadn't previously known about or seen as permissible.

As Barbara told in her spiritual history in chapter 1, the dynamic Youth Week leader did this for her as a teenager. Then, 30 years later, another clergyman became part of her spiritual family tree by asking about her interests and concerns, revealing some of his own, and admitting some of his doubts. Rather than staying behind a mask of piety, he revealed his true self. He let Barbara know that he was also a voracious reader and was interesting in discussing serious subjects and books they both had read. His acknowledgement of Barbara's main interests and abilities helped to convince her that they mattered, in contrast to her previous experience in church and elsewhere, which had told her to stifle and ignore them. He even encouraged her to think that God might be calling her to put her abilities and interests to use in ways she'd never dared to consider before.

For Laura, another member of our class, motivation to reevaluate her beliefs and to see new meaning in the Christian faith came from her grown daughter, Amy. Amy had grown up in the church, but only as a young adult did she realize what Christianity really meant. A Bible study group at work opened her eyes. She reported her new insights and questions to Laura, and as a result, Laura's Christian commitment increased greatly. Hearing about Laura's experience reminded our class members that even our children could function as spiritual ancestors for us. We saw that whoever helps us mature in faith plays that role.

We recognize such people as kindred spirits and cherish them, especially when both we and they see that a real relationship to God and real obedience to God means much more than routine participation in conventional religious institutions. We're fortunate if some of these kindred spirits happen also to be members of our biological family. Even when they aren't, however, we often feel closer to them than to our biological family members. Jesus evidently was acknowledging this when his disciples asked him to leave a teaching session to talk to his mother and brothers outside. "Who is my mother, and who are my brothers?" he responded. "And pointing to his disciples," the Bible tells us, "he said, 'Here are my mother and my brothers! For whoever does the will of my Father in heaven is my brother and sister and mother'" (Matthew 12:46-50).

## The Influence of Open Communication

How do spiritual ancestors exert their influence on us? Our class members saw that most of our spiritual ancestors had influenced us by deliberately and openly communicating their beliefs, interests, and personal experiences. Some did it publicly from a pulpit, a class lectern, or a prominent position in the secular community. Some wrote books or wrote letters to us. Some influenced us by publicly taking unpopular stands on issues or refusing to go along with shady, but common, practices in the church or business world. Sometimes what influenced us was a person's dynamic personality, speaking style, or outstanding achievement. Whether or not these people knew us or had any direct personal contact with us, they revealed something important about what they believed and what they felt their beliefs required them to do.

What often influenced us was someone's taking a special interest in us and spending time with us. Some of our spiritual ancestors merely noticed us and engaged us in conversation. Others invited us to a worship service, Sunday School class, or study group. The owner of a bed-and-breakfast where Arlene lived as a young adult invited her to church. Arlene went, joined that church, and never went back to the denomination she had been in since childhood.

## The Influence of Reading

Barbara's spiritual ancestors include many authors, even though she knows few of them personally and has never seen many of them in person. Some were no longer living when she read their books. When Barbara began thinking about what she believed, *The Edge of Adventure*, by Keith Miller and Bruce Osborne,[1] and Pierre Teilhard de Chardin's *The Divine Milieu*[2] were especially influential. Other books of Miller's influenced her strongly, too, by acknowledging changes that he, as a layman, saw the church needed if it was to be effective in carrying out its God-given purpose. Although Barbara's own observations told her that many of the church's usual practices weren't likely to accomplish that purpose, she had never previously heard anyone in the church admit that.

Other important spiritual ancestors for Barbara were books by Carl Jung and Christian Jungians Morton Kelsey and John Sanford. They helped her make sense of the symbolic language that she had seen in the church and in the Bible for years without realizing its meaning. Although it isn't explicitly religious, *Please Understand Me*, by David Keirsey and Marilyn Bates,[3] is a book that Barbara considers one of her most valuable spiritual ancestors. Understanding the characteristics of different personality types helped her realize that she had God-given gifts, even though they were different from those of most people she knew. Especially at a time when church turmoil made Barbara wonder if there was any real point to the church, by acknowledging and answering some of her questions these and other books helped to change her from a robotlike

churchgoer to one who saw that the church's true purpose was important and that God had a place for her in accomplishing that purpose.

## The Influence of Painful Experiences

Even events that seem negative and painful, like the turmoil that caused Barbara to think about the church's purpose, can become life-changing spiritual ancestors. Sharing her spiritual family tree reminded Anne how the civil rights turmoil of the 1960s had influenced her. After growing up in a rural area with little racial or religious diversity, during her early 20s Anne lived in a city where violent civil rights protests tore apart not only the city but also its churches. For the first time Anne realized how African Americans and Jews were segregated and mistreated, and she was horrified to see churches supporting these conditions instead of taking the lead to get rid of them. That eye-opening experience permanently erased Anne's naive view of the church. It also showed her the important role that promoting justice plays in being a Christian.

A family crisis was a key part of Fran's spiritual ancestry. As a child she was responsible for her little sister during a church service. Her sister went forward during an altar call, and Fran saw no reason to stop her, but their parents were furious at Fran when they found out. It was a sore subject for a long time, but remembering it and thinking about why it happened has led Fran to reevaluate her beliefs and appreciate the church more.

## The Influence of People and Events

The Holy Spirit somehow puts certain people and events in our path and then causes us to notice them. In some cases we knowingly ask God for help and an experience or a person shows up to answer our prayers. In other cases God seems to lead us to the event or person when we didn't even know we were looking for help or needed any.

Influential spiritual ancestors often are people who have deliberately offered themselves to God, signing on to help others. They may have chosen the ordained ministry, for example. Or as lay people they may have taken on volunteer leadership roles in the church, in some other religious organization, or in a charitable organization: as a Scout leader, perhaps, or a youth group sponsor. Still others may have been in professions like teaching. They chose to give guidance but may not necessarily have thought of it as spiritual guidance.

## Thanking Your Spiritual Ancestors

Of people who have served as God's instruments in our lives, some may not know that they played such an important part in our spiritual histories. As Larry told in chapter 1, until Larry presented his spiritual family tree to our Sunday School class, Steve didn't know how valuable Larry had found a comment Steve had made in class years earlier. If the people who have helped you—knowingly or unknowingly—are still living and you haven't ever thanked them, how about thanking them now while you still can?

Telling your children about your spiritual ancestry is important, too. Recording your spiritual family tree can help your descendants know what you contributed to their spiritual ancestry. Anna, a church member in her 80s, has recently drawn her spiritual family tree and written an account of what its various parts mean to her. She has placed her description in the family Bible that she will leave to her children and grandchildren. What a joy her gift will undoubtedly be for them in future years, and even to later generations who will never know Anna except by what she has written.

## Strengthening Your Faith

Spiritual ancestors come in many forms. In addition to members of our biological families they may include teachers, pastors, rabbis, Scout leaders—the possibilities are endless. They may include famous people and some whose names we never knew. They may include books, articles, movies, plays, musical works, and live performances. They may include events that happen to get our attention. Whoever your spiritual ancestors may be, we urge you to let your spiritual family tree help you recall and share them. For good or for ill, they've helped make your faith what it is today. Recalling them may strengthen and deepen it now. In addition to helping groups become stronger communities, sharing spiritual family trees can promote maturity in personal faith.

Sharing our spiritual family trees can also show us ways in which God wants us to take our new insights out into the world and apply them in ways we haven't previously considered. In the last chapter of the book we'll give more attention to how that can happen, in addition to drawing some conclusions about what many of our spiritual family trees have in common.

## Looking Deeper

- To what extent have you made your own religious choices and commitments rather than merely adopting your parents' without ever having examined them closely or considered any others?

- How have people outside your family influenced your religious beliefs or your way of acting on those beliefs?

- Whose religious beliefs or practices are you in a position to influence? How might you need to be more open in making your beliefs known or revealing where you stand on a current issue?

- If you have children, have you made your beliefs known to them and listened to theirs?

- Have communication, painful experiences, reading, and life events helped to clarify your religious beliefs or bring you closer to God?

CHAPTER **8**

# Seeing the Future

Now that we've looked at how genograms originated and how they can help us bring real community to our religious groups, it's time to look to the future. By considering what different people's spiritual family trees seem to have in common, we can get some ideas about what our religious groups need to do and to avoid doing, to help strengthen faith and build community. And by reflecting on our own spiritual trees, we may be able to get some new insights about what our faith means. We may also become aware of ways in which God is calling us to venture out into the world to show others what God is like and how God wants people to live.

## Early Influences

To no one's surprise, members of our Sunday School class saw that our religious habits and attitudes had started early. During childhood most of us had copied our family's religious habits, good or bad. If our parents were regular churchgoers, we were too. If we saw our parents praying, we learned to pray. If they read the Bible openly at home, had daily devotions, or said grace at meals, we took part and assumed that was what everyone was supposed to do. If the Bible was absent from our childhood home or stayed in a bookcase, however, we learned that it wasn't for reading. If no one in our household took part in a church, we got the impression that what churches did was unimportant. If family members and friends continually badmouthed the church or other religious groups or institutions, we assumed these negative evaluations were correct.

For some of us a grandparent or other family member to whom we were especially close had more influence than our parents in starting us on a journey of faith. That person may have read to us, prayed with us, and talked with us about beliefs and values, or he or she may merely have had character traits we admired.

Later in life, experiences beyond our family caused several of us to question and even to abandon the religious habits and attitudes we had seen at home. For many of us, events in the church or in society triggered questioning and change, and people outside our families played key roles in our spiritual growth. In effect, these people and events became our spiritual ancestors, our spiritual family. Many of them eventually had even more influence on our faith than our biological family.

No matter what triggered our thinking, at some time each of our Sunday School class members had started giving deliberate thought to the religious habits and beliefs we had unthinkingly copied from our family during childhood. Some of us decided those habits weren't necessary and discarded them. If we came to feel that regular churchgoing was pointless, we stopped. If we concluded that our family's religious affiliation wasn't right for us, we changed to a different one.

Some of us who had grown up not going to church became churchgoers. Some who had been only occasional attenders became active. Some class members who had been active churchgoers, but hadn't thought much about why, took a fresh look and became active in new ways. Gary, for example, who grew up in a churchgoing family, said, "Church didn't really get a grip on me when I was growing up. It was never a big deal. I sort of liked the Jesus story and some other Bible stories, but that was about it." As a young adult he stayed active in the church, mainly in its social service projects, but only in recent years did he take part in Bible study classes and start reading and thinking seriously about the Bible.

In contrast, other class members had questioned a lot over a long period of time. Some started as teenagers. Others didn't start until midlife. Many dropped out of the church for a while—during college, especially—but then returned to their former pattern with only minor changes. Some members had for a long time been skeptical about what they saw churches doing and about the religious beliefs they heard proclaimed in church. Deep down, for years, they had suspected that some of their church's practices were pointless or inconsistent with the beliefs the church proclaimed. These members had wondered why things they read in the

Bible or heard in church didn't seem to match what they saw happening in their world. They had wondered why people who claimed to be Christians didn't seem to act in ways that matched their talk. But for a long time these class members hadn't had the nerve to question or even mention such things openly. They had assumed that since so many people apparently found these claims convincing, they must somehow be true. Only relatively late in life did these class members dare to ask questions or openly express doubts and to look actively for answers.

Whenever and however it happened, at some point most of us had deliberately examined the faith that others had presented to us. Each of us had arrived at a faith that we saw as "my faith."

For some, finding what we could honestly claim as "my faith" meant change. It meant saying, "The faith that I saw as I was growing up was not really my faith. This other faith is mine." For others, however, arriving at "my faith" meant consciously claiming our parents' faith. We said, in effect, "Their faith is also my faith." These class members who had happily continued their childhood religious patterns without ever seriously questioning them tended to see faith mainly as what their church presented. For them, "my faith" was essentially the same as "my church."

Which of these ways of looking at the religious patterns of your childhood matches your experience? If none of them do, what pattern have you followed in your religious beliefs and practice?

## Copying Our Parents

In sharing our spiritual family trees, some of us were surprised by seeing ways in which, without even realizing it, we have continued some of our parents' ways of acting out their beliefs. For the first time, we recognized some of our attitudes toward the church that are copies of our parents' ways. And we saw that while

some of those are valid and helpful, others aren't.

This awareness came as a surprise even to those of us who had already thought a lot about our parents' influence on us. More than ever, Barbara saw the extent to which she had grown up seeing conventional morality, good manners, and church participation as what being a Christian meant. In presenting her spiritual family tree she saw for the first time the similarity between her recent efforts to promote change in the church and her father's efforts in the '50s to combat church trends that he considered dangerous. The changes he worked for were almost the opposite of those Barbara considers necessary, but his tendency to analyze church practices and work for change was surprisingly similar to Barbara's.

## Continuing to Grow

Describing our spiritual family trees helped us to clarify and become more aware of our beliefs. It's easy to think that you know what you believe and why, we realized, until you try to put it into words.

For most members of our Sunday School class, recognizing and claiming our own faith hasn't been a one-time event. Instead, it has been a continuing process of growth and change. For most of us, in fact, it's still going on. We keep becoming aware of questions or issues or angles that we haven't thought about before. We examine them and sometimes revise or expand our previous beliefs as a result. We all tend to feel that reevaluating our beliefs, seeking more information, and expanding our understanding of God should never stop, because, like all human beings, we can never see all of God or know God's will perfectly. Maybe that's why our class is named the Searchers Class. That doesn't mean we're still looking for God. It means we believe that, because we're finite and God is infinite, we can never see all there is to see of God. There's always more to find.

## Appreciating Our Group and Each Other

In addition to gaining new insights about ourselves, each other, our faith, our spiritual gifts, and the church, our class members became closer to each other and better able to appreciate each other's beliefs and feelings through sharing spiritual family trees. We became more aware of what those beliefs and feelings were and learned which experiences and people had influenced them and how. We're closer now, too, because we now have the common experience of sharing spiritual family trees. We also know that we have experiences, beliefs, and feelings in common.

We saw how influential our actions and words can be, even when we don't realize they're influencing anyone. We especially saw the importance of giving personal attention to someone. Even if we merely serve as a sounding board or provide a listening ear at a crucial time (which we may not know is crucial), especially during that person's youth and young-adult years, we may be making a life-changing contribution to that person's faith.

After seeing the benefits of sharing our family trees, Roberta now wants to do something similar in a non-church group she's in. She and most of the other group members have been meeting for years, and many are friends with other opportunities to be together, but she now realizes that she doesn't know these friends as well as she thought she did or as well as she'd like to.

We also saw our appreciation of the church grow. We saw how disillusioning its failure to practice what it preaches can be, but we also saw how much it has meant to each of us despite its shortcomings.

We became more aware of some of our values, feelings, and attitudes toward the church and other church members. We saw more clearly how specific experiences and people in the church had contributed to our present attitudes, for good and for ill. We saw the importance of getting a broader perspective. We realized that we continually needed to remember that the church was more than the people or practices we happened to have seen. We saw that we needed to recognize Christian tradition as much more than the small part we happened to have seen in our own families and congregations.

As an unexpected bonus, our class attendance improved during our time of sharing. We all hated to miss a single Sunday because being absent meant missing the chance to hear someone's story and thus to know that person and ourselves better.

## Hearing God's Call

The insights that come from sharing spiritual family trees, for leaders and others of us who care about the religious groups we belong to, are many. One is responsibility. In this kind of sharing process leaders need to do more than just bring the pencils and paper, give the instructions, and see that no one monopolizes the conversation. They must be catalysts in their groups. They must nudge the group forward so that it can do God's work more effectively.

This often means helping group members see the need to work for change, not only in themselves but also in the groups and systems they're part of. If as a result of examining and sharing our spiritual family trees we don't learn from our personal experiences and then take what we've learned out into the world, we miss an important discovery, perhaps the message God intended us to hear.

By looking at ourselves and our religious groups in the sharing of spiritual family trees, we can discover not only ways to change our personal behavior but also ways to influence the groups we're in. We can identify actions and events in our churches or other groups that defeat God's purpose and ways that these groups keep their members from using their God-given gifts. We can shine a light on the good and help to overshadow or reverse the bad. We can help our fellow group members feel that they're part of a community.

New awareness is usually God's call to do something. Whenever we learn something new about ourselves, as we're all likely to do when we share spiritual family trees, we make a mistake if we merely conclude, "This is the way I am." We err even further if we then tell our group and the wider world, "Don't expect me to be any different." To follow God's will more closely, new insight should make us see the need for change in either our personal lives or our public lives so that we can work more effectively in the groups we're part of. That insight should also lead us to become, and to help our groups become, more open and sensitive to the wide variety of individuals, God-given talents, and callings within those groups.

We won't have to think very long to identify problems in our religious groups and the wider world that so far seem to defy solutions but that we as people of faith need to address actively. Maybe sharing spiritual family trees can help. What about sharing with people of a different race, a different social class, a different religion, a different country, or a different sexual orientation? If we knew more about what has led each of us to our present beliefs, habits, and feelings, we might be less inclined to let our differences keep us apart or cause us to treat each other unkindly.

## Envisioning a New Future

Looking at our spiritual past can lead us toward a different future. A group that recognizes the wide-ranging influence of past spiritual experiences becomes able to envision new ways of carrying out God's will in the future. By seeing how their past experiences and relationships have led them to their present faith and ministries, group members can begin to believe that what they do in the present can lead to a future they hadn't previously considered possible. It's as if the group collectively visualizes something new into existence.

You can probably think of ministries that have blossomed from the vision of an individual or a small group to become a huge step toward accomplishing a God-given mission. Habitat for Humanity, for example, was envisioned by a few people before it became the far-reaching program it now is. Similarly, Martin Luther King, Jr., and other leading spokespeople of the civil rights movement made us aware of God's call to accept and love people different from ourselves. As a result, in more recent years we have begun to recognize the need not only to continue combating racism but also to see the harm done by sexism and to reexamine our society's attitudes toward gays and lesbians. Becoming aware of how important certain values were to our spiritual ancestors can help us see how to apply those values more extensively in the future.

When members of a religious group feel heard and respected, and when they come to understand how their own spiritual journey relates to the journey of their congregation and their entire faith tradition, they begin to recognize the future path to which God is calling them. It's likely to resemble the path they've followed in the past but to lead them into greater spiritual growth and perhaps to new, God-inspired social or political action.

## Helping Our Groups

We wish that the members of every church or synagogue group, whether it's a class, a choir, a committee, or the bishops, could share their spiritual family trees with each other. Doing so will likely be harder for large groups, for those that meet infrequently, and for those that must transact a lot of business when they meet, but even these groups can find a way. Finding that way will be worth the effort. A retreat is one option. Breaking up a large group into smaller groups for sharing is another.

What if, instead of preaching a traditional sermon, pastors presented their spiritual family trees one Sunday morning? Imagine how much closer congregation members might feel to those pastors. Congregants who understood their pastor's spiritual history might also be more tolerant of his or her human imperfections and views that differ from their own.

If members shared spiritual family

trees with each other, they'd probably become more aware of what their churches need to be doing. They'd realize the long-lasting damage done by ineffective pastors, boring church activities, and apathetic, silent lay members. They'd also see the positive influence that dynamic leaders, challenging classes, lively members, and exciting worship can have. Members might even see that, as lay people, they don't always need special training, professional leaders, or official permission to do a lot of what needs doing in their church and other religious groups.

Wouldn't these results benefit all religious organizations? We believe they would. Through sharing spiritual family trees, we can see how trees of many different kinds make up the forest that is our religious tradition. Sharing faith stories can help to increase faith, empower group members, and build community. Our Sunday School class and numerous other groups have found that sharing spiritual family trees is an especially effective way of doing that. We heartily recommend it to you.

## Looking Deeper

- When the future members of your religious group look at their spiritual histories and the part today's members played in them, what do you think they will say?

- Based on what you and your group have seen in your spiritual history, what do you see God calling you to do now and in the future?

- How could you and your group make that calling a reality?

**Chapter 2**
    1. Monica McGoldrick, Randy Gerson, and Sylvia Shellenberger, *Genograms: Assessment and Intervention* (New York: W.W. Norton, 1999).
    2. Marsha Wiggins Frame, "The Spiritual Genogram in Family Therapy," *Journal of Marital and Family Therapy* 26, no. 2 (April 2000): 211.
    3. Daniel C. DeArment, *Journal of Pastoral Care* 41, no. 2 (June 1987): 114.
    4. Edwin H. Friedman, *Generation to Generation: Family Process in Church and Synagogue* (New York: Guilford Press, 1985).

**Chapter 3**
    1. Frederick A. Norwood, *The Story of American Methodism* (Nashville: Abingdon Press, 1974), 130.
    2. Ibid., 132
    3. James R. King Jr., *The Kentucky Conference NetNews*, January 2001.
    4. John Patton, *Pastoral Care in Context: An Introduction in Pastoral Care* (Louisville, Ky.: Westminster/John Knox Press, 1993), 15.
    5. Charles Gerkin, *An Introduction to Pastoral Care* (Nashville: Abingdon Press, 1997), 36.
    6. Pamela Couture, *Blessed Are the Poor: Women's Poverty, Family Policy and Practical Theology* (Nashville: Abingdon Press, 1991), 25.

7. Peter L. Steinke, *How Your Church Family Works: Understanding Congregations as Emotional Systems* (Bethesda, Md.: The Alban Institute, 1993), ix–xi.

8. Ibid., 4.

9. Edwin H. Friedman, "Foreword" in Steinke, *How Your Church Family Works,* vi.

10. Gil Rendle, telephone conversation with Barbara Wendland, 21 March 2001.

11. Walter Wink, *Unmasking the Powers: The Invisible Forces That Determine Human Existence* (Philadelphia: Fortress Press, 1986), 69–70.

12. Wink, *The Powers That Be: Theology for a New Millennium* (New York: Galilee/Doubleday, 1998), 4.

13. Ibid., 6.

14. Rendle, telephone conversation.

**Chapter 4**

1. Frame, "Spiritual Genogram," 213.

2. Ibid., 214.

**Chapter 6**

1. David Keirsey and Marilyn Bates, *Please Understand Me: Character and Temperament Types* (Del Mar, Calif.: Prometheus Nemesis Books, 1978).

2. David Keirsey and Marilyn Bates, *Please Understand Me II: Temperament, Character, Intelligence* (Del Mar, Calif.: Prometheus Nemesis Books, 1998).

3. Corinne Ware, *Discover Your Spiritual Type: A Guide to Individual and Congregational Growth* (Bethesda, Md.: The Alban Institute, 1995).

4. Lynne M. Baab, *Personality Type in Congregations: How to Work with Others More Effectively* (Bethesda, Md.: The Alban Institute, 1998).

**Chapter 7**

1. Keith Miller and Bruce Osborne, *The Edge of Adventure: An Experiment in Faith* (Waco, Tex.: Word Books, 1974).

2. Pierre Teilhard de Chardin, *The Divine Milieu* (New York: Harper & Row, 1960).
3. Keirsey and Bates, *Please Understand Me.*

# BIBLIOGRAPHY

Baab, Lynne M. *Personality Type in Congregations: How to Work with Others More Effectively.* Bethesda, Md.: The Alban Institute, 1998.

Couture, Pamela. *Blessed Are the Poor: Women's Poverty, Family Policy and Practical Theology.* Nashville: Abingdon Press, 1991.

DeArment, Daniel C. *Journal of Pastoral Care* 41, no. 2 (June 1987): 114.

de Chardin, Pierre Teilhard. *The Divine Milieu.* New York: Harper & Row, 1960.

Frame, Marsha Wiggins. "The Spiritual Genogram in Family Therapy," *Journal of Marital and Family Therapy* 26, no. 2 (April 2000): 211–16.

Friedman, Edwin H. *Generation to Generation: Family Process in Church and Synagogue.* New York: Guilford, 1985.

———. "Foreword" in Steinke, Peter L. *How Your Church Family Works: Understanding Congregations as Emotional Systems.* Bethesda, Md.: The Alban Institute, 1993.

Gerkin, Charles. *An Introduction to Pastoral Care.* Nashville: Abingdon Press, 1997.

Keirsey, David, and Marilyn Bates. *Please Understand Me: Character and Temperament Types.* Del Mar, Calif.: Prometheus Nemesis Books, 1978.

———. *Please Understand Me II: Temperament, Character, Intelligence.* Del Mar, Calif.: Prometheus Nemesis Books, 1998.

King, James R., Jr. *The Kentucky Conference NetNews*, January 2001.

McGoldrick, Monica, Randy Gerson, and Sylvia Shellenberger. *Genograms: Assessment and Intervention.* New York: W.W. Norton, 1999.

Miller, Keith, and Bruce Osborne. *The Edge of Adventure: An Experiment in Faith.* Waco, Tex.: Word Books, 1974.

Norwood, Frederick A. *The Story of American Methodism.* Nashville: Abingdon Press, 1974.

Patton, John. *Pastoral Care in Context: An Introduction in Pastoral Care.* Louisville, Ky.: Westminster/John Knox Press, 1993.

Rendle, Gil. Telephone conversation with Barbara Wendland, 21 March 2001.

Richardson, Ronald A. *Creating a Healthier Church: Family Systems Theory, Leadership, and Congregational Life.* Philadelphia: Fortress Press, 1996.

Steinke, Peter L. *How Your Church Family Works: Understanding Congregations as Emotional Systems.* Bethesda, Md.: The Alban Institute, 1993.

Ware, Corinne. *Discover Your Spiritual Type: A Guide to Individual and Congregational Growth.* Bethesda, Md.: The Alban Institute, 1995.

Wink, Walter. *Unmasking the Powers: The Invisible Forces That Determine Human Existence.* Philadelphia: Fortress Press, 1986.

———. *The Powers That Be: Theology for a New Millennium.* New York: Galilee/Doubleday, 1998.